SUMMER 2011 ■ VOLUME 34 NUMBER 3

THE
WASHINGTON QUARTERLY

5 PROVOCATIONS

7 A Military Strategy for the New Space Environment
■ *William J. Lynn, III*

In less than a generation, space has fundamentally and irrevocably changed. The Deputy Secretary of Defense outlines the National Security Space Strategy, charting how the United States will seek to maintain a strategic advantage despite the more complicated environment.

17 The Climate Wars Myth
■ *Bruno Tertrais*

The stakes of climate change are important, but history shows that it is not an essential factor to explain collective violence, nor are "water wars" or floods of "climate refugees" on the horizon. Climate change is simply not a meaningful factor for defense and security planning.

31 Germany as a Geo-economic Power
   ■ *Hans Kundnani*

   Germany is emerging as not just a civilian power, but a pure
   example of a geo-economic power. Berlin has become more
   willing to impose its economic preferences, but is once again
   reluctant to use military force, even under UN auspices for
   humanitarian purposes in Libya.

47 Al-Qaeda and the Rise of China: Jihadi Geopolitics in a
    Post-Hegemonic World
   ■ *Brian Fishman*

   China will undoubtedly play a larger role in Osama bin
   Laden's successors' reassessment of the global geopolitical
   picture. Beijing, in turn, must determine how its traditional
   foreign policy should evolve to respond to the increasing
   problems posed by al-Qaeda and its allies.

63 China and the United Nations: The Stakeholder Spectrum
   ■ *Michael Fullilove*

   In the past quarter-century, China has become a far more
   active and effective player in the UN, sometimes even
   outperforming the United States. Yet, the last five years have
   defined more clearly the limits of Beijing's conversion: China
   wants respect, but not responsibility.

87 Crimea's Overlooked Instability
   ■ *William Varettoni*

   Crimea is far more complex, and at risk of civil conflict, than
   most recognize, and Russia is not the problem. Ethnic
   tensions, a widening Islamic–Orthodox Christian fissure,
   disinformation campaigns, and cycles of elite-manipulated
   instability all threaten a downward spiral of civil violence.

101 The Road Ahead

103 The Battle for Reform with Al-Qaeda
■ *Juan C. Zarate and David A. Gordon*

Paradoxically, the Arab Spring represents a strategic pivot for al-Qaeda and its associated movements—at once the moment is an existential threat to its ideology and a potential window to restore lost relevance amidst its core Sunni constituency and its concept of reform-by-jihad.

123 Israel's Pessimistic View of the Arab Spring
■ *Daniel Byman*

Dismissing Israel's doom-and-gloom mentality is too easy. Some of its fears are valid, and others that are less so will still drive Israeli policies. Yet in the end, for Israel to decry the winds of change sweeping the region risks missing opportunities to nudge it in the right direction.

137 Beware the Duck Test
■ *Bruce W. Jentleson*

Historically, four strategic miscalculations have shaped U.S. views of major regional events like recent change in the Arab world and led to policy failures. While learning the right lessons won't assure success, not learning them makes failure more likely.

151 The Trust Deficit: Seven Steps Forward for U.S.–Arab Dialogue
■ *Mina Al-Oraibi and Gerard Russell*

A pan-Arab journalist and a former British spokesperson to global Muslim audiences sketch seven principles for the United States, still uniquely capable of influencing regional events, to help win the war of ideas in the Middle East.

Provocations

A new military strategy for space ... the climate wars
myth ... al-Qaeda and China ... and much more

William J. Lynn, III

A Military Strategy for the New Space Environment

As disaster struck Japan and revolution swept the Middle East, Americans once again watched events unfold in real time, through a network of satellites in space that have revolutionized the dissemination of information and changed how we live. For decades, we have taken this network, and the operational environment of space which supports it, for granted. But quietly, almost imperceptibly, revolutions of a less visible kind have been unfolding above us in space itself. Over the Middle East, censorship imposed by autocratic states has for the first time extended into the upper reaches of the atmosphere. The satellite-based telecommunications services of Thuraya—a regional satellite phone provider—have been disrupted, and the satellite broadcasts of Al Jazeera, the Voice of America, and the BBC rendered unintelligible. Libya and Iran are the primary offenders, but even less technologically developed countries such as Ethiopia have employed jamming technologies for political purposes.

The willingness of states to interfere with satellites in orbit has serious implications for our national security. Space systems enable our modern way of war. They allow our warfighters to strike with precision, to navigate with accuracy, to communicate with certainty, and to see the battlefield with clarity. Without them, many of our most important military advantages evaporate.

The specter of jamming is not the only new concern. The February 2009 collision of an Iridium communications satellite with a defunct Soviet satellite, and the earlier, deliberate destruction of a satellite by China, produced thousands of debris fragments, each of which poses a potentially catastrophic threat to operational spacecraft. In an instant, these events—one accidental, the other purposeful—doubled the amount of space debris, making space operations more complicated and dangerous.

William J. Lynn, III is the U.S. Deputy Secretary of Defense.

Copyright © 2011 Center for Strategic and International Studies
The Washington Quarterly • 34:3 pp. 7–16
DOI: 10.1080/0163660X.2011.586933

Without space systems, many of our most important military advantages evaporate.

In less than a generation, space has fundamentally and irrevocability changed. Unlike the environment we knew for the first 50 years of the space age, space is now characterized by three "C's": it is increasingly congested, contested, and competitive. These changes not only pose tremendous technical challenges to military space systems, they also force rethinking of how we use space to maintain our national security. The National Security Space Strategy released on February 4, the first ever of its kind, establishes a new approach to space.[1] Building upon emerging norms of behavior and a renewed commitment to share capabilities with allies and partners, the strategy charts how we will maintain our strategic advantage despite the more complicated environment.

Congested

In 1957, at the dawn of the space age, there was just one man-made object in space—the Soviet satellite Sputnik. Today, more than 1,100 active systems and 22,000 pieces of man-made debris orbit earth (Figure 1). Eleven states now

Figure 1: Source: Joint Space Operations Center

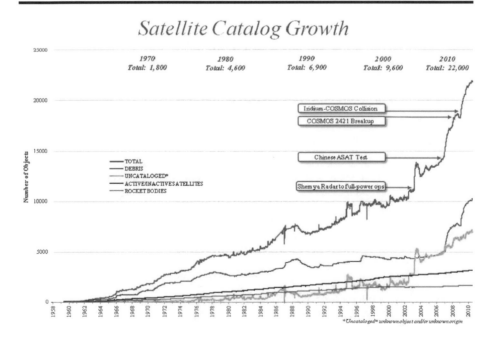

Satellite Catalog Growth

operate 22 launch sites, and more than 60 nations have a presence in space. Not only has the number of objects in space grown, but the rate at which they materialized also has increased dramatically. It took 40 years to place the first 10,000 objects in outer space, and a mere 10 years to place the next 10,000 in orbit. Hundreds of thousands of additional

Space is increasingly congested, contested, and competitive.

pieces of debris remain too small to track with our current sensors. Whether or not we can see it, the debris is there. The danger is that each collision exponentially raises the potential for another, such that a debris cascade could someday render entire orbits unusable. Scientists today debate how soon the tipping point will be reached. More immediately, debris can instantly knock out capabilities on which both our military and the global economy rely.

Space is also cluttered by electronic signals. Roughly 9,000 satellite transponders that send communications between space and the ground are expected to be active by 2015, increasing the probability of radio frequency interference. Military planners are keenly aware that a satellite does not need to be physically damaged to be rendered useless—it only has to be jammed, intentionally or otherwise. The dramatic increase in physical and electronic hazards means we are approaching a point at which the limitless frontier no longer seems quite so limitless.

The Obama administration has already taken notice. The president's National Space Policy, a landmark document issued in 2010, declares that the sustainability, stability, and free access to space are vital national interests.[2] To help bring order to this congested environment, the United States is promoting the responsible use of space. Along with the right to use and explore space comes the responsibility to be a good steward of it.

In 2007, the UN General Assembly approved guidelines to mitigate the creation of space debris. But how to operate safely in space needs to be further defined. The United States is working with the European Union on a proposed international Code of Conduct for Outer Space Activities. These guidelines would lay down "rules of the road" and allow the international community to hold accountable those who break them. Rules of the road for space can serve a similar purpose as maritime guidelines at sea—increasing safety for all operators and reducing the risk of dangerous incidents.

The Pentagon is also taking a hard look at how its own policies can help foster a more cooperative space environment. Just this year, we broadened our pre-launch notification policy to include space launch vehicles, rather than just ballistic missile launches. We hope that increasing our own transparency will encourage other space-faring nations to act responsibly when conducting space operations.

The 2011 National Security Space Strategy establishes a new approach to space.

In addition to rules, guidelines, and confidence-building measures, we are expanding our sharing of information regarding situational awareness in space. For years, the United States has provided data on the location of space objects to the global community, so that operators of space systems can avoid accidental collisions. The Secretary of Defense recently signed statements of principles with Australia, Canada, and France that lay the groundwork for expanding this cooperation. Further expanding the amount and kind of data we share will, over time, help foster the sustainable space environment that our own strategic advantage depends upon.

Contested

During the Cold War, space largely remained the private preserve of the United States and the Soviet Union, with space assets as tools of superpower control. Missile warning and imagery satellites enabled us to detect missile launches and to verify the arms control arrangements meant to lessen the risk of conflict. During this period, each nation developed hit-to-kill, anti-satellite weapons that had the potential to generate large clouds of space debris. Since the space domain was inextricably linked with our understanding of nuclear escalation, the employment of such weapons was believed to serve as the harbinger of a nuclear first-strike.

Although in the past information derived from space capabilities went almost exclusively to national decisionmakers, today we rely on space for almost everything we do. Space systems are critical to operations on the ground, at sea, and in the air, whether enforcing a no-fly zone over Libya or countering insurgents in Afghanistan. With such widespread reliance comes potential vulnerability. A greater number of potential adversaries now employ a wider spectrum of weapons capable of countering U.S. space capabilities. As a result, physically shooting down a satellite is no longer the most likely threat to our military systems.

Electronically jamming GPS and communications signals are among a range of relatively low-cost options for states seeking counterspace weapons. The threshold for using these weapons has been lowered, with a number of nations employing them for political purposes in peacetime or during crises. For example, Iran has recently jammed the BBC's Persian television service in an effort to limit information about regional unrest. Furthermore, counterspace weapons are no longer the weapon of last resort in a geo-strategic conflict. Instead, they are becoming tools that advanced nations and sub-regional powers alike are incorporating into conventional military doctrine. Even non-state actors have found utility in employing jammers and manipulating communications satellites. For instance, the Tamil Tigers in Sri Lanka have been accused of hijacking transponders on commercial communications satellites to broadcast propaganda, demonstrating a sophisticated understanding of space technology. Irregular warfare has come to space.

To respond to the proliferation of counterspace weapons, the United States is employing new ways to prevent and deter aggression against U.S. and allied space systems. In the contested space environment of today, we can no longer rely solely on the threat of retaliation to protect space systems from attack. We must expand our traditional concepts of deterrence. Accordingly, the National Security Space Strategy outlines the multilayered approach we will take to deter aggression. This approach includes several important initiatives.

First, we are assessing diplomatic initiatives such as the EU Code of Conduct to promote international norms of responsible behavior. These initiatives define how responsible space-faring nations are expected to conduct themselves and should over time discourage destabilizing acts that threaten the overall stability of the space domain. Nations willfully acting contrary to such norms can expect to be isolated as rogue actors.

Second, we can utilize alliances in space to serve the same deterrent function as basing troops in allied countries. They can ensure an attack on one is an attack on all. As with terrestrial defense alliances, partnerships in space also can add resilience and capabilities, without relinquishing the strategic advantage our systems provide. At their fullest, these partnerships could consist of completely interoperable systems in which costs, benefits, and risks are shared among trusted participants. For instance, Australia recently became a full partner in the Wideband Global Satellite Communications System (WGS), which directly supports warfighters. The cost-savings from our partnership with Australia allowed the Pentagon to procure an additional satellite for the WGS constellation. By sharing the benefits and risks of developing this system, we enhanced our operational capability and raised the cost of aggression against it.

Increasingly, we will want to operate in coalitions in space, just as we do in other domains. To achieve this, the department will examine all mission areas to identify where shared interests open the door to greater levels of cooperation. One way to foster greater cooperation is to transform the Joint Space Operations Center, which provides command and control for our space forces, into a Combined Space Operations Center run in concert with international partners. Such an arrangement will allow our partners to work side-by-side with U.S. commanders, improving our situational awareness while integrating a multilateral approach to day-to-day operations. Networking our space operations center with those of our allies offers a further way to expand collaboration. But even as we increasingly work in partnerships, we will maintain some U.S.-only capabilities for our most sensitive national security missions.

Third, we need to make our space systems more resilient, and our combat power less reliant on their full functioning. This will help deny adversaries the benefit from an attack in space. Just as in the cyber domain, denying the benefit of attack in space can join retaliatory deterrence as a disincentive to adversaries. To maintain our combat power, we are learning how to operate in a degraded information environment. Training exercises where we disrupt space-based capabilities help our forces become proficient at operating with interference. To improve resiliency, we are developing technology to help us mitigate the loss or degradation of on-orbit systems. For instance, we now have ground, air, and naval-based platforms which can increasingly augment or replace space assets. The U.S. military is one of the few militaries today with the capability to operate in all domains on a global basis, and this ability provides a strategic advantage when space capabilities come under threat.

Responsive space capabilities which rapidly launch replacements can also play an important role in reconstituting functionality either during or after an attack. And broader partnerships with commercial firms which enable national security payloads to ride on commercial satellites will further improve our resiliency. Hosting military payloads on commercial spacecraft, as we are already doing with a missile warning sensor, is not only cost-effective, it also enables a more diverse, robust, and distributed set of space systems.

Finally, the United States views free access to space as a vital national interest. Consistent with our inherent right of self-defense, we will respond accordingly to attacks on it, at a time and place of our choosing—and not necessarily in space. Ultimately, deterrence must impact the decision-making of particular countries and leaders in specific scenarios. A multilayered approach to deterrence offers the greatest likelihood of encouraging restraint, and thereby protecting our vital space capabilities from attack.

Competitive

Addressing the congested and contested environment is not the only challenge to maintaining our strategic advantage in space. Our nation's fiscal climate and the globalization of the aerospace industry also present new challenges. As noted, today there are more than 60 nations with satellites. Many of these nations have a national aerospace industry, presenting both challenges and opportunities for greater collaboration and partnership.

During the Cold War, the technological supremacy of the U.S. industrial base enabled the Pentagon and the Intelligence Community to field systems much more advanced than those of the Soviet Union. Although the United States continues to enjoy technological leadership, our share of satellite manufacturing has steadily declined since the end of the Cold War (Figure 2; note that 2009 appears to be an anomaly because of the unusually large number of spacecraft delivered to replenish commercial satellite fleets). As a result, advanced capabilities are more diffuse. For example, the precise navigation and timing data transmitted by the U.S. Air Force-operated Global Positioning System (GPS) is a capability that will soon be replicated by Europe's Galileo, Russia's Glonass, China's Beidou, Japan's Quasi Zenith, and India's Regional Navigation System. More broadly, space-enabled information and services that were once the exclusive province of the national security community are now available commercially. Satellite imagery distributed by companies like Google and satellite communications—such as phones and radio broadcasts—can be purchased globally. The U.S. technological lead is eroding in other areas as well, and without immediate intervention, the vitality of our space industrial base is at risk.

To ensure we maintain world-class space capabilities at affordable costs, the Pentagon must alter how it buys space systems. Our current approach of procuring one satellite at a time creates unpredictable demand, fostering a boom-

Figure 2: Source: Satellite Industry Association

Notes: Revenue figures are in-year estimates, not adjusted for inflation over time. Satellite Manufacturing revenues are recorded in the year the satellite is delivered/launched, not when contract is awarded or interim payments are transacted. World revenue includes U.S. revenue.

Without immediate intervention, the vitality of our space industrial base is at risk.

and-bust dynamic unhelpful to accumulating manufacturing and design expertise. So we are adopting a new approach to space acquisition meant to drive down costs and improve the stability of the space industrial base. Key tenets of this approach are block buys of satellites, fixed price contracting, stable investment in research and development, and a modified annual funding approach. The Pentagon plans to work with Congress to gain authority to implement this strategy for upcoming procurement of Advanced Extremely High Frequency (AEHF) communications satellites and Space-Based Infrared System (SBIRS) missile warning satellites. Our hope is that increasing the predictability of how we buy and manufacture space systems will yield both cost-savings and performance increases.

Change must also stretch beyond the Department of Defense, to the regulations that govern what our space industry is allowed to export. Presently, many items generally available on the global market for space commerce are prohibited from being sold by U.S. companies without government approval. Our current export policy puts us in a double bind. We are hurting our own space suppliers in the international market and are not really impeding states of concern from acquiring sensitive space technologies. To redress the current state of affairs, the administration is undertaking export control reform. The foundation of the new regime is to consolidate responsibility for export control into a single licensing agency, a single tiered list of controlled items, a single coordination center for enforcement, and a single, unified IT infrastructure. We recognize that controlling sensitive space exports remains a concern. So we are building "higher fences" around our most sensitive technologies, while de-listing those items whose export does not threaten our security.

The global spread of space technology in the last 20 years, and the related restructuring of our own space industry, is a development we can no longer ignore. The companies who manufacture our space systems are the source of innovation that has helped us maintain our leadership in space for more than half a century. To ensure their continued viability in the global market, we must change how we regulate the export of technology and how we buy space systems.

A New Type of Leadership

Space has fundamentally changed, and our national security strategy must change along with it. Today, our relationship to potential adversaries is very different from our past stance toward the Soviet Union. Throughout the Cold War and for some years beyond, the United States focused almost exclusively on protecting the national security advantages we derived from space. We now must also worry about protecting both the domain itself and our industrial base. Our security depends on the integrity of both.

Our new National Security Space Strategy addresses the changing nature of space by building on our sources of strength at home, while continuing to lead the international community in pursuit of common objectives, including the sustainability, stability, and free access to space. Our success will increasingly be predicated on active U.S. leadership of alliance and coalition efforts in peacetime, crisis, and conflict. Strengthening our space posture will follow an approach that integrates all elements of national power, from technological prowess and industrial capacity to alliance building and diplomatic engagement.

Maintaining our ability to use space to influence the course of military and political situations will require many actions. We must reconsider what capabilities we develop, how to employ them, and what kind of partnerships to build into our systems. We must also ensure the stability of the space domain, expand how we protect space systems in a contested environment, and alter how we acquire space systems. The National Security Space Strategy builds on these tenets. But devising a strategy is only the first step. We must also execute it successfully.

Although space is central to our national security, the mechanisms in the Department of Defense that set priorities and oversee long-term planning have become diffused. Especially as we bring our policies, programs, and acquisition strategies into alignment around the elements I believe are essential to a new strategy, we need to manage space in a more effective manner. To provide the necessary leadership, we are revalidating the Secretary of the Air Force as the Executive Agent for Space. This administrative designation makes clear to everyone who is in charge. We have also established a Defense Space Council to coordinate space issues across the department. Our expectation is that better governance inside the department will lead to stronger capabilities, greater efficiencies, and a healthier space industrial base.

Given the dramatic changes we have witnessed in space, succeeding in the new space environment will depend as much on changing mindsets 50 years in the making as it will on altering longstanding institutional practices. The fundamental mission of the Department of Defense to deter war and to protect the security of our country stays the same. But how we use space capabilities to achieve this mission must change.

Notes

1. "U.S. National Security Space Strategy–Unclassified Summary," January 2011, http://www.defense.gov/home/features/2011/0111_nsss/docs/NationalSecuritySpaceStrategyUnclassifiedSummary_Jan2011.pdf.
2. "National Space Policy of the United States of America," June 28, 2010, http://www.whitehouse.gov/sites/default/files/national_space_policy_6-28-10.pdf.

Bruno Tertrais

The Climate Wars Myth

The first decade of the 21st century was the hottest since the beginning of the Industrial Revolution. Global warming is real and, if present trends continue, its possible effects worry publics and governments around the world. Could it foster armed conflict for resources such as food and water? Will Western armies be increasingly called upon to mitigate the effects of natural catastrophes, humanitarian disasters, and floods of refugees?

Think tanks have enthusiastically embraced this new field of research, and militaries around the world are now actively studying the possible impact of a warming planet on global security. Books with titles such as *Climate Wars* predict a bleak future.[1] A well-known French consultant claims that a five degree Celsius increase in average global temperature would generate no less than a "bloodbath."[2] Former World Bank economist Lord Nicholas Stern—the author of the 2006 "Stern Report" on the possible economic impact of climate change—even declares that failing to deal with climate change decisively would lead to "an extended world war."[3]

However, there is every reason to be more than circumspect regarding such dire predictions. History shows that "warm" periods are more peaceful than "cold" ones. In the modern era, the evolution of the climate is not an essential factor to explain collective violence. Nothing indicates that "water wars" or floods of "climate refugees" are on the horizon. And to claim that climate change may have an impact on security is to state the obvious—but it does not make it meaningful for defense planning.

Dr. Bruno Tertrais is a Senior Research Fellow at the Fondation pour la recherche stratégique (Foundation for Strategic Research), and a *TWQ* editorial board member. He may be reached at b.tertrais@frstrategie.org.

Copyright © 2011 Center for Strategic and International Studies
The Washington Quarterly • 34:3 pp. 17–29
DOI: 10.1080/0163660X.2011.587951

What History Teaches Us

Since the dawn of civilization, warmer eras have meant fewer wars. The reason is simple: all things being equal, a colder climate meant reduced crops, more famine and instability.[4] Research by climate historians shows a clear correlation between increased warfare and cold periods.[5] They are particularly clear in Asia and Europe, as well as in Africa.[6] Interestingly, the correlation has been diminishing since the beginning of the Industrial Revolution: as societies modernize, they become less dependent on local agricultural output.[7]

Moreover, if there was any significant link between warfare and warming, the number of conflicts should have been rising in the past two decades. It has not—quite the contrary. Since the end of the Cold War, the total number of wars, after having steadily increased since 1945, has diminished. Statistics published by the Stockholm International Peace Research Institute (SIPRI), which come from work done at the Uppsala University, clearly show such a decrease. Today, there are half as many wars as two decades ago (17 in 2009 versus 35 in 1989).[8] This result is mainly due to the rapid decrease in the number of internal conflicts.[9] As with the number of interstate conflicts, civil wars began to decline from the end of the 1970s onwards. Classic international war has, statistically speaking, disappeared from the modern world. According to the SIPRI/Uppsala University data, in 2009, for the sixth year in a row, there was no ongoing interstate war. (Iraq and Afghanistan do not belong to that category.) Such conflicts represented, in the 2000s, three out of a total of 30 wars, thus 10 percent of the total—in a world where the number of states has tripled since the end of the Second World War.

There is even a reverse correlation. The average global temperature diminished between 1940 and 1975: during that period, the total number of conflicts was on the rise. Correlation is not causation. (It may be tempting to argue that the modernization of societies leads to two separate, parallel outcomes: global warming *and* global peace.) But the existence of these data points should contribute to extreme caution about the hypothetical equation according to which a warmer world would be a war-prone world.

In 2007, the Nobel Peace Prize was attributed jointly to the Intergovernmental Panel on Climate Change (IPCC) and to former U.S. Vice President Al Gore. Rarely was the attribution of a Nobel Peace Prize so blatantly out of sync with geopolitical realities.

A Flawed Concept

Of course, some local changes of the climate can have an impact on the stability of societies, and thus increase the propensity to collective violence, generally in a marginal way and mostly in developing countries. Such is the case, for instance, for droughts in countries which are heavily dependent on rain-fed agriculture.[10] But drawing deterministic conclusions from this observation would be a stretch. There are examples the other way round. At the border of Kenya and Somalia, conflicts are more numerous when the resource (pastures) is abundant.[11] This fits with a well-known pattern. Resource-rich countries are more likely to be involved in conflict: oil, minerals, or timber attract predators, and revenues from their exploitation fuel civil war.

Darfur is the poster child of "climate conflict." It is appropriate to consider that local variations of climate and the natural environment in western Sudan were part of the conditions that led to collective violence in the region. But they were not a key reason or root cause.[12] For if that were the case, how would one explain that conflict erupted nearly 30 years after the current period of drought began? Moreover, the conflicts that took place in the Sahel region in the 1970s clearly show that political and human factors are the key to understanding most if not all wars. In that region, the two preceding decades (the 1950s and 1960s) had seen abundant precipitations; local governments had then deliberately encouraged the development of agriculture in steppes, something which moved cattle-raising toward the north. When rain decreased, cattle-raisers sought to reclaim their lands, but faced farmers who were battling the drought. These tensions happened against the background of a traditional rivalry between nomads and settlers, which was frequently instrumentalized by local or national governments. And in northern Mali, the Tuareg rebellion would probably not have happened without the radicalization of young Malians who had emigrated to Algeria or Libya because of the drought.[13] Human and political factors trump climate and environmental ones.

> Variations of the climate were not a root cause of conflict in Darfur.

In seeking to demonstrate that climate change will lead to more instability, experts sometimes stretch causality chains to the breaking point. A good example is the recent attempt by two researchers of the International Institute for Strategic Studies to show that climate change played a significant role in the Arab Spring of 2011.[14] According to them, extreme weather events of 2010—record rainfall in Canada, droughts in the former Soviet Union, a cyclone in Australia—led to an increase in food prices, which in turn fueled discontent in the Middle East. But there are three problems with their proposition. First, there is no evidence that the 2010 events deviated so much from traditional weather patterns in these regions that they had to be attributed to climate change. Second, as the authors themselves acknowledge, other factors were at play behind the spike in food prices, such as speculation or the demand for biofuels. Third and most importantly, while food prices may have played a role in the Arab discontent, the authors offer no evidence for their contention that they played a "necessary" role.

Most experts of the links between the environment and conflict refrain from adhering to dire predictions about impending climate wars. They show extreme caution about what the historical record shows regarding those links, which are deemed to be at best "highly speculative."[15] A careful review of the issue concludes that "the concept of environmentally induced conflict is itself fundamentally flawed."[16] More precisely, as explained by two researchers, "the suggested causal chains from climate change to social consequences like conflict are long and fraught with uncertainties. One could ask whether it is indeed conceptually fruitful to be talking about climate change and conflict at all."[17]

Talking about "climate wars" is not only unsubstantiated—it may be harmful. When United Nations Secretary-General Ban Ki-moon, along with others, claims that climate change is probably one of the key causes of the Darfur conflict, those who perpetrated the massacres should applaud, for it partly absolves them of their own responsibilities. Environmental security expert Geoffrey Dabelko argues "Characterizing climate change as producing a new type of conflict is both wrong and counterproductive. For instance, simply labeling the genocide in Darfur a 'climate war' ignores political and economic motivations for the fighting—and unintentionally could let the criminal regime in Khartoum off the hook."[18]

Beware of Catastrophic Scenarios

Some of the most catastrophic scenarios of climate change-induced conflict just do not stand up to scrutiny. To study the possible political consequences of changes in the geography of the Arctic region due to climate change is one thing. To imagine this could lead to armed clashes between Russia and the North Atlantic Treaty Organization (NATO) is another. First, the diminution of the maximum extent of summer sea ice will not transform the North-Western Passage and the Northern Maritime Route into vital maritime trade arteries: they will be open only a few weeks or a few months a year. Second, the real quantity of hydrocarbon resources in the region is still very much open to debate; and such resources are, for the most part, located within national maritime areas. Third, the attitude of all neighboring states regarding this region, including Russia, reflects a clear preference for settling possible disputes in accordance with accepted international law. Fourth, the scope of these disputes is not increasing—rather the opposite: in April 2010, Norway and Russia settled their decades-long dispute on the delimitation of their respective maritime areas in the Barents Sea.

The interruption of the North Atlantic Conveyor Belt ("Gulf Stream") due to global warming is a favorite of thrillers and science-fiction writers. The study of its consequences by a consulting firm at the request of the U.S. Department of Defense's Office of Net Assessment a few years ago was widely noted.[19] The problem is that the credibility of this scenario is close to nil. Recent scientific research has shown that the Gulf Stream is animated much less by thermohaline circulation (differences in the temperature and salinity of water) than by the winds. Moreover, its role in shaping and regulating the climate of Northern Atlantic regions has been seriously put in doubt.[20]

Finally, the argument according to which global warming will lead to an increase in the number of natural catastrophes, with grave humanitarian consequences, should be taken with a heavy pinch of (marine) salt. The only available evidence that global warming will lead to more extreme weather events relies on modeling. Data do not really sustain this hypothesis so far. There has not been any increase in global precipitation in recent decades.[21] Neither have droughts become more frequent or severe.[22] Hurricane activity is not stronger, and its variation remains within the range of natural variation.[23] The number of hurricane events has tended to evolve downwards since 1970; in accumulated intensity, 2010 was its lowest in 30 years.[24]

> Talking about "climate wars" is not only unsubstantiated—it may be harmful.

The Emergency Events Database (EM-DAT) maintained at the Leuwen University in Belgium—one of the most widely used databases for natural disasters—shows a clear rise in the number of weather-related catastrophes over the last 30 years. However, this rise can easily be explained by demographic, economic, sociological, and political factors. EM-DAT only takes into account events that have caused a significant number of victims (which is rising due to population increase and the growing number of humans living on exposed areas), for which a state of emergency has been declared, and a call to international help has been made (the frequency of which is rising for political and media reasons).[25] Furthermore, the number of reported catastrophes has also increased—as compared to what it was say, a century ago—due to improved detection and attention. There is every reason to believe that the human, social, and economic consequences of natural catastrophes will be increasingly severe, but this has little to do with climate change.

It should also be noted that natural disasters do not necessarily have only negative consequences on national and international security. Quite the contrary: disasters appear to *prevent* rather than promote civil conflict.[26] A case in point is the 2004 Asian tsunami, which indirectly contributed to the stabilization of the decades-old secessionist conflict in the Indonesian province of Aceh (a peace agreement was signed in August 2005).

No Wars Over Water

An avatar of the notion of climate war is that of future wars over water. Such wars have been forewarned since the late 1980s, but the theme has gained popularity since the end of the Cold War.[27] If some commentators are to be believed, "the lines of battle are already being drawn for the water wars of the future."[28] It is true that the map of predicted water stress at the 2025–2030 horizon reveals a close match with the map of major geopolitical risks: the Arabian Peninsula and Central Asia are among the regions which are most likely to be affected.

Warming will not change anything about the global availability of water resources, but will probably induce changes in the geographical distribution of precipitation. However, this will not necessarily be for the worse: in many regions, the resource for agriculture will increase.[29] Other regions will see more droughts. However, recent studies have shown that climate change—whatever its origin—has only a small part of responsibility for water crises: population increase is by far the main cause.[30]

Will the melting of Himalayan glaciers lead to a severe water crisis in South Asia, one of the most dangerous parts of the world? On this point, the IPCC included a serious error in its 2007 report, due to a series of confusions. The text claims that these glaciers could be reduced by 80 percent in 2035. The date came from a 2005 report by the World Wildlife Fund (WWF), for which primary sources were press articles and unpublished communications. (The WWF report now includes a correction retracting its claims.)[31] As to the proportion of glaciers which could disappear by that time, it came from a 1996 UNESCO Report, which mentioned a possible 80 percent reduction of the global total of non-polar ice (not just Himalayan glaciers), but by the year 2350, not 2035.[32] Resorting to non-peer-reviewed publications is also what led the IPCC to wrongly claim, based on an unsubstantiated assertion included in the Stern Report, that water availability in South Asia was highly dependent on glacier melt.[33] But recent studies have shown that Himalayan glacier melt accounts for only three to 25 percent of the

> Climate change has only a small responsibility for water crises; population increase is the main cause.

volume of rivers in South Asia: monsoons and local seasonal snow melt are by far their main sources.[34]

And water crises do not mean water wars. The issue of access to water resources is undoubtedly a major dimension of numerous regional crises, in particular in the Greater Middle East, as testified by decades-old disputes between Turkey and Syria, or Egypt and Sudan. The value of strategic locations such as the Golan Heights or Kashmir is not a small part of tensions between Syria and Israel, or India and Pakistan. And water sharing can be the cause of local disputes sometimes degenerating into small-scale collective violence in Africa or Asia. However, experts from the University of Oregon, who maintain the most complete database on this topic, state that there has never been a "war over water" (that is, large-scale collective violence for the sake of a water resource) in the past 4,500 years.[35] The last war over water opposed two Sumerian cities in the middle of the third millennium B.C.E., about sharing the waters of the Tigris and Euphrates. There are good reasons for such a scant record. Any country seeking to control the upstream of a river would need to ensure complete and permanent domination over it, which would be an ambitious goal. In the modern era, resorting to arms over water (like resorting to arms over oil) is just not worth the cost. Especially for those whose geographical location and budget can afford to build desalination plants—which is the case for some of the most water-stressed countries, those located on the Arabian Peninsula.

One should therefore not be surprised that access to water has always generated more cooperation than conflict. Since antiquity, thousands of agreements and treaties have been signed for water-sharing. And cooperation between adversaries has stood the test of wartime, as was seen during the 20th century in the Middle East, South Asia, or Southeast Asia.

Climate Barbarians at the Gates?

What about "climate refugees"? Dire evaluations already existed in the middle of the 1990s: British environmentalist Norman Myers claimed at the time that such refugees already numbered 25 million, and that their number might double 15 years later, to reach perhaps 200 million by the middle of the century. This number has been used by many publications since then.[36] Another widely-quoted prevision—which claims to be an update of Myers' own—is that of the non-governmental organization Christian Aid, which foresees 250 million climate refugees between 2007 and 2050 (out of a total of one billion environmental refugees).[37] Lord Stern himself reportedly stated that a five degree Celsius rise in average global temperature would lead to "billions" having to move.[38]

Waves of refugees triggered by climate change does not square well with the reality of migration.

But the idea of massive waves of refugees triggered by climate change does not square well with the reality of migration. There is no doubt that environmental change can lead to massive displacements of populations. Such displacements have always existed, including in industrialized countries. Remember the Dust Bowl, which led to the migration of two to three million from the Great Plains to the West in the United States. But such movements are slow (we are more accurately talking about migrants as opposed to refugees), very much dependent on economic opportunities existing elsewhere (the "pull" factor is as important as the "push"), and generally of a limited geographical scope (most people want to stay in the same country or region).[39] They are sometimes due to non-climate related factors: desertification or degradation of the soils is often due to urbanization or intensive agriculture.

The same reasoning can be applied to the rise in sea levels. First, the hypothesis of a future constant rise in average sea levels due to global warming is not the likeliest one and is being seriously challenged.[40] Second, even if one accepts the scenario of a constant rise, is it inconceivable that mankind would be able to adjust and adapt to a rise of a few millimeters per year, as it has done for many decades? Catastrophist analyses evoking massive floods of refugees do not square well with an average rise of two to six millimeters a year (the range of IPCC scenarios). And given such a slow pace, some countries will balance the rise of sea level mass by sedimentation. Take the example of Bangladesh, a poster child of the possible consequences of climate change. The idea that the densely populated coastal regions of that country could be flooded by the rise in sea levels does not take into account the parallel accumulation of sediments brought by the great South Asian rivers, which amount to about one billion metric tons a year.[41]

Such are the reasons why experts of environmental migrations generally agree that climate change in itself is rarely a root cause of migration.[42] Major population displacements due to environmental and/or climatic factors will remain exceptional except in the case of a sudden natural disaster.[43] And most importantly for the sake of this analysis, they are rarely a cause of violent conflict.[44]

It is not even certain that the very concept of "climate refugees" is relevant.[45] Atmospheric or hydrological catastrophes can create massive—and most of the time temporary—population displacements. But such catastrophes have always existed. Why then attempt to create a separate category for their victims, which would distinguish them from those of geological catastrophes (earthquakes, tsunamis, volcanic eruptions) for which human activities bear no responsibility? The concept of climate refugees says more about Western fears of "barbarians at the gates" than it does about the foreseeable reality of the consequences of climate change.[46]

Is Climate Change Even Relevant to Defense Planning?

So much for "climate wars." But the idea according to which climate change is nevertheless a new, important factor to be taken into account in defense and security planning is itself questionable. Of course, nothing precludes us from including it in the growing list of non-military issues that may have a bearing on global security. But this has to be done in a realistic way. It is not unreasonable to state that climate change may be a "threat multiplier," for instance.[47] However, stating this says nothing about the probability of increased violence or instability either at the global level or for a given crisis, or about the likelihood of state failure. Such consequences depend primarily on the reaction of governments and societies—a factor which is impossible to calculate in advance.

There are no data to support the vague idea that climate change can have a key role in triggering collective violence—that is, be the proverbial straw that breaks the camel's back, as argued by an alarmist study (citing once again the example of Darfur).[48] Climate is "one of myriad factors in a complex causal web underlying conflict," and the environment is just "one of manifold and non-essential causal factors" which may lead to war.[49] The main causes of contemporary conflict are societal, not natural (in the broadest sense of the term, i.e., including man-made).[50] Conflicts are borne out of human choices and mistakes.

Could regional previsions of the impact of climate change at least inform policymakers and planners about the areas of the world which are more likely—all things being equal—to suffer from them? The answer is no. Regional effects are extremely difficult to predict with the degree of probability which can be useful for planning.[51] The IPCC itself underscores that current models do not have the ability to deliver useful previsions at a higher scale than the continental one.[52] Nobody knows, for instance, whether African monsoons will move northwards (with positive effects on agriculture) or southwards (with negative effects). Here, as noted by a contributor to the IPCC, "there is complete disagreement between the various models."[53] And when the IPCC attempts to give regional previsions on the evolution of agricultural output, for instance, it is in a way which does not buttress the case for alarmism. Its 2007 report mentions a possible reduction by 50 percent of rain-fed agricultural output in some African countries in 2020. But the sole source it cites to support this claim is a report produced for a Canadian non-governmental organization in which it is mentioned that (unpublished) studies evoke this scenario for three Maghreb countries.[54]

There are indeed, it seems, some causal links between climate and warfare. But they are of a seasonal nature: "nations address seasonal climate change in terms of where they fight, rather than through when or whether disputes occur. . . . Fighting moves to higher latitudes in the summer, and lower latitudes during the cooler months of the year."[55]

The stakes of climate change are important—and that is why this area should not be the object of intellectual fantasies or fashions. It is appropriate for defense and security planners to monitor the evolution of the scientific and political debate on its possible consequences. But there is no objective reason today to list climate change as a key issue for defense and security planning.

Notes

1. Gwynne Dyer, *Climate Wars* (Toronto: Random House, 2008); Harald Welzer, *Klimakriege: Wofür im 21. Jahrhundert getötet wird* (Frankfurt: S. Fischer Verlag, 2008).
2. Jean-Marc Jancovici quoted in Antoine Robitaille, "Les changements climatiques: vers la guerre?" *Le Devoir*, November 19, 2009.
3. Quoted in Charles J. Hanley, "Lord Nicholas Stern Paints Dire Climate Change Scenario: Mass Migrations, Extended World War," The Huffington Post, February 21, 2009, http://www.huffingtonpost.com/2009/02/21/lord-nicholas-stern-paint_n_168865.html.
4. Richard S.J. Tol and Sebastian Wagner, "Climate change and violent conflict in Europe over the last millennium," *Climatic Change* 99 (2010): pp. 65–79, http://metapress.com/content/e78581pv740rx500/fulltext.pdf
5. David D. Zhang et al., "Global climate change, war, and population decline in recent human history," *Proceedings of the National Academy of Sciences* 104, no. 49 (2007), http://www.pnas.org/content/104/49/19214.full.pdf+html.
6. David D. Zhang et al., "Climatic change, wars and dynastic cycles in China over the last millennium," *Climatic Change* 76 (2006), pp. 459–477; Zhibin Zhang et al., "Periodic climate cooling enhanced natural disasters and wars in China during AD 10-1900," *Proceedings of the Royal Society—Biological Sciences* 277 (2010): pp. 3745–3753, http://rspb.royalsocietypublishing.org/content/277/1701/3745.full.pdf+html; Halvard Buhaug, "Climate not to blame for African civil wars," *Proceedings of the National Academy of Sciences* 107, no. 38 (2010), http://www.pnas.org/content/107/38/16477.full.pdf+html.
7. Tol and Wagner, "Climate change and violent conflict in Europe over the last millennium."
8. Stockholm International Peace Research Institute (SIPRI), SIPRI Yearbook 1989–2009.
9. Stathis N. Kalyvas and Laia Balcells, "International System and Technologies of Rebellion: How the Cold War Shaped Internal Conflict," *American Political Science*

Review 104, no. 3 (August 2010), http://stathis.research.yale.edu/documents/Kaly
vas_Balcells_APSR.pdf.

10. Edward Miguel et al., "Economic Shocks and Civil Conflict: An Instrumental Variables Approach," *Journal of Political Economy* 112, no. 4 (2004), http://www.econ. berkeley.edu/~emiguel/pdfs/miguel_conflict.pdf.

11. "Climate Wars," *The Economist*, July 8, 2010.

12. Michael Kevane and Leslie Gray, "Darfur: Rainfall and Conflict," *Environmental Research Letters* 3, no. 3 (July–September 2008), http://iopscience.iop.org/1748-9326/3/3/034006/fulltext.

13. Tor A. Benjaminsen, "Does Supply-Induced Scarcity Drive Violent Conflicts in the African Sahel? The Case of the Tuareg Rebellion in Northern Mali," *Journal of Peace Research* 45, no. 6 (November 2008), http://jpr.sagepub.com/content/45/6/819.abstract.

14. Sarah Johnstone and Jeffrey Mazo, "Global Warming and the Arab Spring," *Survival* 53, no. 2 (April–May 2011).

15. Clionadh Raleigh and Henrik Urdal, "Climate Change, Environmental Degradation and Armed Conflict," *Political Geography* 26, no. 6 (2007): pp. 7–8.

16. Tobias Hagmann, "Confronting the Concept of Environmentally-Induced Conflict," *Peace, Conflict and Development* 6, no. 6 (January 2005): p. 4.

17. Ragnhild Nordås and Nils Petter Gleditsch, "Climate Conflict: Common Sense or Nonsense?" Human Security and Climate Change Workshop, Oslo, June 21–23, 2005, p. 24, http://waterwiki.net/images/d/d8/Nordas_Gleditsch.pdf.

18. Geoffrey D. Dabelko, "Avoid hyperbole, oversimplification when climate and security meet," Bulletin of the Atomic Scientists, August 24, 2009, http://www.thebulletin.org/web-edition/op-eds/avoid-hyperbole-oversimplification-when-climate-and-security-meet.

19. Peter Schwartz and Doug Randall, "An Abrupt Climate Change and Its Consequences for United States National Security," Global Business Network, October 2003, http://www.gbn.com/articles/pdfs/Abrupt%20Climate%20Change%20February%202004.pdf.

20. Richard Seager et al., "Is the Gulf Stream responsible for Europe's mild winters?" *Quarterly Journal of the Royal Meteorological Society* 128, no. 586 (October 2002), http://www.ldeo.columbia.edu/res/div/ocp/gs/pubs/Seager_etal_QJ_2002.pdf; Richard Seager, "The source of Europe's mild climate," *American Scientist* 94, no. 4 (July–August 2006).

21. Thomas M. Smith et al., "Variations in annual global precipitation (1979–2004), based on the Global Precipitation Climatology Project 2.5 analysis," *Geophysical Research Letters* 33 (March 18, 2006).

22. Justin Sheffield et al., "Global and Continental Drought in the Second Half of the Twentieth Century: Severity-Area-Duration Analysis and Temporal Variability of Large-Scale Events," *Journal of Climate* 22, no. 8 (April 2009): pp. 1962–1981.

23. Thomas R. Knutson et al., "Tropical cyclones and climate change," *Nature Geoscience* 3 (February 21, 2010): pp. 157–163.

24. Ryan N. Maue, "Global Tropical Cyclone Activity," Center for Ocean-Atmospheric Prediction Studies, Florida State University, http://www.coaps.fsu.edu/~maue/tropical/.

25. See http://www.emdat.be/.

26. Rune Slettebak and Indra de Soysa, "High Temps, High Tempers? Weather-Related Natural Disasters & Civil Conflict," Draft Paper for the Conference on Climate Change and Security, Conference of the Royal Norwegian Society of Sciences and Letters, Trondheim, June 21–24, 2010, http://climsec.prio.no/papers/Slettebak%20and%20de%20Soysa%20-%20Temp%20and%20Temper.pdf.

27. Joyce R. Starr, "Water Wars," *Foreign Policy* 82 (Spring 1991): pp. 17–36, http://www.ciesin.org/docs/006-304/006-304.html.

28. Colin Mason, *A Short History of the Future: Surviving the 2030 Spike* (London: Earthscan, 2006), p. 62.

29. Nigel W. Arnell et al., "Climate change and global water resources: SRES emissions and socio-economic scenarios," *Global Environmental Change* 14, no. 1 (April 2004): pp. 31–52.

30. Matti Kummu et al., "Is physical water scarcity a new phenomenon? Global assessment of water shortage over the last two millennia," *Environment Research Letters* 5, no. 3 (July–September 2010).

31. World Wildlife Fund (WWF) Nepal Program, "An Overview of Glaciers, Glacial Retreat and Subsequent Impacts in Nepal, India and China," March 2005 [with correction], http://www.panda.org/downloads/climate_change/glacierssummary.pdf.

32. Vladimir M. Kotlyakov, ed., "Variations of Snow and Ice in the past and at present on a Global and Regional Scale," UNESCO, 1996, http://unesdoc.unesco.org/images/0010/001065/106523e.pdf.

33. Intergovernmental Panel on Climate Change (IPCC), "Climate Change 2007: Impacts, Adaptation and Vulnerability," Chapter 10, "Asia," http://www.ipcc.ch/pdf/assessment-report/ar4/wg2/ar4-wg2-chapter10.pdf.

34. Pallava Bagla, "No Sign Yet of Himalayan Meltdown," *Science* 326, no. 5955 (November 13, 2009): pp. 924–925; Walter W. Immerzeel et al., "Climate Change Will Affect the Asian Water Towers," *Science* 328, no. 5984 (June 11, 2010): pp. 1382–1385.

35. Jerome Delli Priscoli and Aaron T. Wolf, *Managing and Transforming Water Conflicts* (New York: Cambridge University Press, 2009).

36. Norman Myers, "Environmental refugees in a globally warmed world," *BioScience* 43, no. 11 (December 1993): pp. 752–761; Ibid., "Environmental Refugees," *Population and Environment* 19, no. 2 (November 1997): pp. 167–182.

37. Christian Aid, "Human Tide: The Real Migration Crisis," May 2007, http://www.christianaid.org.uk/Images/human-tide.pdf.

38. Quoted in Hanley, "Lord Nicholas Stern Paints Dire Climate Change Scenario: Mass Migrations, Extended World War."

39. Cecilia Tacoli, "Not only climate change: mobility, vulnerability and socio-economic transformations in environmentally fragile areas in Bolivia, Senegal and Tanzania," International Institute for Environment and Development, February 2011, http://pubs.iied.org/10590IIED.html.

40. Paleo Sea Level Working Group, "The sea-level conundrum: case studies from palaeo-archives," *Journal of Quaternary Science* 25, no. 1 (January 2010): pp. 19–25.

41. "Bangladesh gaining land, not losing: scientists," Agence France-Presse, July 30, 2008, http://www.terradaily.com/reports/Bangladesh_gaining_land_not_losing_scientists_999.html.

42. Elisabeth Meze-Hausken, "Migration Caused by Climate Change: How Vulnerable Are People In Dryland Areas?" *Mitigation and Adaptation Strategies for Global Change* 5, no. 4 (2000): pp. 379–406.

43. Clionadh Raleigh et al., "Assessing the Impact of Climate Change on Migration and Conflict," The Social Development Department, World Bank, undated, http://siteresources.worldbank.org/EXTSOCIALDEVELOPMENT/Resources/SDCCWorking Paper_MigrationandConflict.pdf.

44. Ibid.

45. Richard Black, "Environmental refugees: myth or reality?" New Issues in Refugee Research, Working Paper no. 34, United Nations High Commissioner for Refugees, March 2001, http://www.unhcr.org/research/RESEARCH/3ae6a0d00.pdf.

46. Cecilia Tacoli, "Crisis or adaptation? Migration and climate change in a context of high mobility," Prepared for Expert Group Meeting on Population Dynamics and Climate Change, UNFPA/International Institute for Environment and Development, June 24–25, 2009, http://www.unfpa.org/webdav/site/global/users/schensul/public/CCPD/papers/Tacoli%20Paper.pdf.

47. Kurt M. Campbell et al., "The Age of Consequences: The Foreign Policy and National Security Implications of Global Climate Change," Center for Strategic and International Studies / Center for a New American Security, November 2007, http://csis.org/files/media/csis/pubs/071105_ageofconsequences.pdf.

48. "National Security and the Threat of Climate Change," CNA Corporation, 2007, http://securityandclimate.cna.org/report/National%20Security%20and%20the%20Threat%20of%20Climate%20Change.pdf.

49. Jeffrey Mazo, "Climate Conflict: How global warming threatens security and what to do about it," International Institute for Strategic Studies, Adelphi Paper no. 409, March 2010, p. 40, p. 12, p. 40.

50. Raleigh and Urdal, "Climate Change, Environmental Degradation and Armed Conflict."

51. Demetris Koutsoyiannis et al., "On the credibility of climate predictions," *Hydrological Sciences Journal* 53, no. 4 (August 2008).

52. IPCC, "Climate Change 2007: Synthesis Report—Summary for Policymakers," p. 10, http://www.ipcc.ch/pdf/assessment-report/ar4/syr/ar4_syr_spm.pdf.

53. Quoted in Sylvestre Huet, "Des temps incertains," *Libération*, November 13, 2007.

54. Ali Agoumi, "Vulnerability of North African Countries to Climatic Change: Adaptation and Implementation Strategies for Climate Change," International Institute for Sustainable Development, 2003, http://www.iisd.org/cckn/pdf/north_africa.pdf.

55. Erik Gartzke, "Does Climate Change Whether, When or Where Nations Fight?" Paper prepared for the Climate Change and Security Conference, Royal Norwegian Society of Sciences and Letters, Trondheim, June 21–24, 2010, p. 1, p. 28, http://climsec.prio.no/papers/climate_for_conflict_06202010.pdf.

Hans Kundnani

Germany as a Geo-economic Power

Berlin's March 2011 abstention on the UN Security Council vote on military intervention in Libya has raised questions about Germany's role in the international system. By abstaining on Security Council Resolution 1973, Germany broke with its Western allies and aligned itself with the four BRIC countries: Brazil, Russia, India, and China. Whether or not the decision signals a weakening of what Germans call the *Westbindung*, it illustrates the strength of Germany's ongoing reluctance to use military force as a foreign-policy tool even in a multilateral context and to prevent a humanitarian catastrophe. Over the past few years, as the number of German and civilian casualties has increased in Afghanistan, the German public has become more skeptical about the mission of the International Security Assistance Force (ISAF) in particular and about the deployment of German troops abroad in general.[1] Like Germany, other EU member states such as France and the United Kingdom are cutting their defense budgets, but Germany shares few of their aspirations to project power beyond Europe.

The abstention was particularly striking—and, for many people, surprising—because it follows a period in which Germany had appeared to become more assertive in its use of economic power within Europe. Under huge pressure from the German public, which blamed others for the eurozone crisis and fears the creation of a "transfer union" (in other words a European Union in which fiscally responsible member states pay for fiscally irresponsible ones), Chancellor Angela Merkel last spring was initially reluctant to bail out Greece, which was in danger of defaulting. She then insisted on tough conditions for the rescue package that was eventually agreed to in May, including the involvement of the International Monetary Fund. Some saw in Merkel's response to the Greek crisis

Hans Kundnani is Editorial Director at the European Council on Foreign Relations. He can be reached at hans.kundnani@ecfr.eu.

Copyright © 2011 Center for Strategic and International Studies
The Washington Quarterly • 34:3 pp. 31–45
DOI: 10.1080/0163660X.2011.587950

a return to classical German great power politics. For example, the former Chancellor Helmut Schmidt accused the German government of "Wilhelmine pomposity" in its attitude towards France, to whom Germany has during the last year tended to dictate.[2] Meanwhile, according to Le Monde, President Nicolas Sarkozy told a friend that the Germans "haven't changed."[3]

However, as the threat from the crisis moved from the periphery closer to the center of Europe in the second half of last year, Germany was paradoxically also criticized for showing too little "leadership."[4] When it became apparent that the creation of the European Financial Stability Fund in May was not enough to reassure the bond markets, Germany came under increasing pressure to put its weight behind a major reform of eurozone economic governance. But, as Germany opposed various proposals that involved greater Europe-wide coordination of economic policy, it was criticized not so much for being expansionist as for being provincial. The philosopher Jürgen Habermas, for example, wrote of "the solipsistic mindset of this self-absorbed colossus in the middle of Europe."[5] In short, allusions by some to the Kaiserreich notwithstanding, it hardly seems as if Germany wants to become a great power again.

The central difficulty of explaining German foreign policy is how to understand this apparent contradiction between the harder edge of Germany's pursuit of national interest within Europe and its continuing—and perhaps even increasing—reluctance to use military force or even to project power in a traditional sense in the wider world. The foreign policy of the post-reunification "Berlin Republic" increasingly seems to be qualitatively different from that of the pre-reunification "Bonn Republic." But Germany is not simply returning to a pre-World War II mode of power—not least because the nature of power in international relations and particularly within Europe has changed so much since then. Rather, Germany seems to be emerging as a particularly pure example of a new form of power in international relations: a geo-economic power.

Germany as a "Civilian Power"

The Federal Republic has traditionally been understood as a "civilian power"— that is, one that, unlike a great power, uses multilateral institutions and economic cooperation to achieve its foreign-policy goals, avoids the use of military force except in limited circumstances and in a multilateral context, and thus helps to "civilize" international relations by strengthening international norms. The term—which is both descriptive and prescriptive—was coined by political analyst François Duchêne in the early 1970s to describe the European Union, and was subsequently applied to Germany and Japan by international relations professor Hanns W. Maull. In a 1990 Foreign Affairs essay, Maull wrote that Germany and Japan had become "prototypes" of "a new type of international power" that accepted the necessity of cooperation with others in the pursuit of international objectives, concentrated on non-military and in particular on economic means to secure foreign-policy goals, and was willing to develop supranational structures to address critical issues of international management.[6]

Maull argued that Germany and Japan had become civilian powers largely by necessity rather than choice. Both defeated in World War II, they were forced to make territorial concessions, but because of the emergence of the Cold War, it would not have been in their national interest to make any territorial demands because it would have undermined stability. In the Cold War context, Germany and Japan also both renounced an autonomous security policy in favor of reliance on the United States—a relatively cheap and effective solution to their defense problems which allowed them to focus instead on economic growth. In short, the Federal Republic did not adopt a civilian power identity in an act of altruism. Rather, it did so because it saw it as the best way of achieving its own post-war foreign-policy ambitions and objectives.

As Maull himself acknowledged, the concept of a civilian power was in many ways similar to that of the "trading state" that Richard Rosecrance had developed a few years earlier.[7] Rosecrance argued that in the 1970s and 1980s, driven by the "the declining value of fixed productive assets," states for whom a traditional strategy was no longer feasible, either because of size or their recent experience with conflict, had increasingly adopted strategies based on augmenting their share of world trade rather than traditional military power or territorial expansion. As a result, there had emerged "a new political prototype" of states that sought their vocation through international commerce rather than territorial expansion. Other foreign-policy analysts have specifically applied the concept of a trading state to Germany.[8]

However, although civilian powers like Germany were in practice often also trading states, civilian powers differ conceptually from trading states in terms of their ultimate objective. In particular, Maull's version of civilian power was very much influenced by the sociologist Norbert Elias' theory of the civilizing process in politics and society.[9] For Maull, the overriding foreign-policy objective of a civilian power is not simply to improve economic performance or prosperity but to civilize international relations through the development of the international rule of law. In other words, a civilian power aims to make international politics like domestic politics. In particular, by avoiding the use of force except collectively and with international legitimacy, it aims to help develop a multilateral monopoly on the use of force analogous to the state's domestic monopoly.

Although the concept of civilian power was meant to describe an ideal position, it proved useful in explaining German foreign policy after 1990. Some, both in and outside Germany, had feared that after reunification, Germany would once again pursue territorial expansion and return to the use of traditional military power politics. In other words, the period of the division of Germany would turn out to be an aberration and the traditional "German question" would once again re-emerge. In fact, however, nothing of the sort happened. Rather, under Helmut Kohl, Germany remained committed to the European integration process which had begun in the 1950s. In 1992, Germany signed the Maastricht Treaty, which completed the creation of a single European market and laid the foundation for the European Monetary Union and, along with it, abolished another aspect of national sovereignty. This seemed to bear out Maull's argument that Germany had changed so much—in particular, it now defined its national interest in terms of integration and interdependence—that a return to the old policies had become impossible.

An important shift did take place in German security policy during the 1990s. After the Gulf War in 1991, Germany came under increasing pressure from its NATO allies, particularly the United States, to play a more active role in resolving conflicts around the world. In response, it took a series of small steps toward greater involvement in international peacekeeping missions. Initially there was a constitutional obstacle: Article 87a of the Basic Law prevented German troops from taking part in "out-of-area" operations. But in 1994, the Constitutional Court ruled that Germany could take part in out-of-area operations provided they were sanctioned by the United Nations and were specifically approved by the *Bundestag*. German troops subsequently took part in UN peacekeeping and eventually combat operations in the Balkans.

This shift in German policy on the use of force culminated in the Kosovo war in 1999, in which Gerhard Schröder's center–left "red–green" coalition agreed to send four German Tornado bombers on missions over Serbia as part of the NATO military intervention—the first major combat mission in the history of the Federal Republic. For Germany, this was a huge step, and was preceded by a tortuous and emotive debate focused largely on German identity after Auschwitz. Unlike previous operations in which German troops had been involved, Operation Allied Force did not have a mandate from the UN Security Council. However, like the previous steps taken in the 1990s toward greater use of military force, the decision to send troops into combat had taken place in a multilateral framework—indeed, it had been at the request of NATO allies—and could be seen as contributing to, rather than undermining, "civilizing" international relations. A decade after reunification, therefore, Germany's civilian power identity seemed as strong as ever.[10]

The Weakening of Germany's "Civilian Power" Identity

During the last decade, however, Germany's civilian power identity has weakened. In particular, Germany has begun to break with this identity in two important ways. First, it has become less multilateral. Although the Federal Republic's multilateralism was always "attritional"—in other words, it was a way to achieve its foreign-policy objectives, above all sovereignty and reunification—this approach was so successful that over the years it became a kind of reflex for the German foreign-policy establishment.[11] During the last decade, however, there has been a shift to a more contingent multilateralism.

Perhaps the most dramatic break with multilateralism came in 2002 when Gerhard Schröder declared that Germany would not support the Iraq war regardless of what was decided at the UN Security Council—a uniquely unilateral action in the history of the Federal Republic up to that point.[12] Although the rhetoric has softened since Angela Merkel took over as chancellor in 2005, the less instinctively multilateral approach begun by Schröder has continued. A striking example was foreign minister Guido Westerwelle's call to remove U.S. nuclear weapons from Germany last year. Instead of negotiating the removal of the weapons through the North Atlantic Council, NATO's decisionmaking body, as other countries such as Greece have done, he chose to make the demand publicly, apparently in order to win points with German voters. (That this approach came not from a left-wing party but from the leader of the Free Democrats, the party of Helmut Kohl's foreign minister Hans-Dietrich Genscher, illustrates the extent to which German foreign policy has changed.)

While Germany now seeks more power within multilateral institutions (for example, since the time of the Schröder government, Germany has actively sought a permanent seat on the UN Security Council), it has become less willing to transfer sovereignty to them. In the case of the European Union, this is partly because of an increase in popular euroscepticism. According to an opinion poll in January, only 41 percent saw Europe as Germany's future, down from 53 percent the previous April.[13] The judiciary has also become more eurosceptic. In a landmark decision in June 2009, the *Bundesverfassungsgericht*, Germany's constitutional court, approved the Lisbon Treaty but also imposed limits on the further transfer of sovereignty to Brussels in a long list of policy areas including security, fiscal, and social policy.[14]

These changes in public opinion and the attitude of the constitutional court reflect a deeper structural shift in Germany's role in the world. Put simply, Germany no longer needs multilateral institutions in the way it used to. For example, it relies on NATO much less than it did during the Cold War, when West

> Germany no longer needs multilateral institutions the way it used to.

Germany was dependent on the alliance for its security. In short, Germany is less constrained than it used to be, and this new freedom means that it can be more selectively multilateral. It now operates through multilateral institutions when it suits it to do so, and bilaterally when it does not.

Similarly, now that Germany has achieved reunification, elites do not perceive European integration as an existential imperative in the way they used to. Although Germany's export economy still needs European markets—60 percent of German exports still go to the eurozone—its trade is increasingly with emerging economies outside Europe. In particular, German exports to China grew by more than 70 percent in the 18 months from the beginning of 2009 to mid-2010. Goldman Sachs has projected that, if these trends remained unchanged for the next 18 months, exports to China would be roughly at the same level as exports to France by the end of 2011. Meanwhile, as enlargement has made it harder to coordinate EU policy with France, it is increasingly tempting for Germany to pursue bilateral "special relationships" with other powers such as China and Russia instead.

> Since reunification, German elites do not perceive European integration as imperative.

The removal of its pre-reunification constraints has allowed Germany to increasingly define its national interest in economic terms. In a sense, this has actually further strengthened Germany's identity as a trading state. Before reunification, the Federal Republic had eschewed military power, but had nevertheless pursued some traditional foreign-policy objectives. In particular, it sought territorial expansion in the limited sense that it sought reunification, although it pursued this objective through multilateral cooperation and economic power. With reunification, however, Germany has become "strategically saturated."[15]

At the same time, the costs of reunification have put Germany under greater economic pressure and therefore made it harder for Germany to pursue other non-economic foreign-policy goals. In particular since Schröder took over as chancellor in 1998, the chancellery has become more active in promoting the interests of business, for example by bringing large trade delegations on visits abroad. Business then has exerted significant influence on key elements of German foreign policy: energy companies like E.ON Ruhrgas have influenced policy towards Russia; automakers such as BMW have influenced policy towards China; and manufacturers of technology and machinery such as Siemens have influenced policy towards Iran.

At the same time, however, a second, subtle shift has also taken place that has to do with the *way* Germany uses its economic power since the European single currency was created in 1999. Since the creation of the euro, the imbalances between eurozone economies, in particular between countries with trade surpluses (for example, Germany) and countries with trade deficits (such as Greece), have grown. As one economist has put it, "the structural differences between a low-inflation, slow growing core and higher inflation periphery were supposed to narrow following the introduction of the single currency. In reality, these differences grew."[16] Between 1997 and 2007, Germany's trade surplus with the rest of the eurozone went from €28 billion to €109 billion, almost quadrupling. In the decade since the creation of the euro, Germany's economy has become "structurally reliant on foreign demand for its growth."[17]

These imbalances, and in particular the increasing dependence of Germany on exports, have led to a perception of a divergence of interests within the eurozone, which came to a head in 2010 after the economic crisis turned into a sovereign debt crisis in member states on the European periphery such as Greece and Ireland. Because Germany tends to blame others for the crisis and see its own economy as a model, it refuses to take steps to reduce its reliance on export growth or to loosen monetary policy, despite being urged to do so by other member states. Germany has been accused of imposing deflationary pressures on the eurozone that may help to maintain the competitiveness of its own exports but could make it harder for debtor countries to grow their way out of recession—what George Soros has called a "Procrustean bed."[18] As a result, many in southern European member states increasingly see Germany as a rival rather than a partner.[19]

Of course, Germany is not solely to blame for this shift from cooperation to competition within the eurozone. Nevertheless, economic *cooperation*—and the transfer of sovereignty as a pre-condition of this—is a key characteristic of a civilian power or trading state. It appears, however, that Germany is not only increasingly defining its national interest in economic terms, but also increasingly using its economic power to impose its own preferences on others in the context of a perceived zero–sum competition within the eurozone, rather than to promote greater cooperation in a perceived win–win situation.[20] Given these shifts, it has become harder to claim that Germany still "civilizes" international relations in the way Maull suggested. The concept of civilian power is still valid as a normative concept; however, it no longer adequately describes Germany as a foreign-policy actor.

Normality and Germany

Although it is becoming increasingly clear that Germany's civilian power has weakened, it is much harder to describe the kind of foreign-policy actor that Germany has become. One concept that has been used to try to capture the shift in German foreign policy since reunification is "normality." Germany, it is suggested, is becoming more "normal." The concept of normality—often opposed to the idea of a German *Sonderweg*, or special path—has been associated with the Berlin Republic since its inception. Like the concept of civilian power, it is both descriptive and prescriptive: most of those who use it support the perceived shift in German foreign policy that they are attempting to capture. However, it is difficult to define a "normal" foreign policy in a clear and meaningful way. Those who apply the concept to German foreign policy usually define normality by referring to France and the United Kingdom—two states that are comparable to Germany in size but have their own particularities arising from their own geographies and histories.[21] For example, unlike Germany, both have extensive former colonies, a nuclear deterrent, and a permanent seat on the UN Security Council (the concept of normality is therefore often used by those who support Germany's bid for a Security Council seat).

Unsurprisingly, because normality is such a problematic concept, it is often used inconsistently. In particular, it is not clear whether the pre-unification Bonn Republic—and many of the aspects of German foreign policy associated with its civilian power identity—should be regarded as "normal" or "abnormal." In one sense, the Federal Republic pursued an "abnormal" foreign policy prior to reunification because of its commitment to multilateralism and economic cooperation rather than military force. In another sense, however, it pursued a "normal" foreign policy because it committed to the West and broke with the tradition of the *Sonderweg*. Those who use the concept of normality in a prescriptive sense often want to have it both ways: they argue for a German foreign policy that is more like that of France and the United Kingdom in terms of selective multilateralism and the pursuit of narrowly-defined national interests, but do not accept that, given Germany's unique geography and history, this undermines the *Westbindung*.

> In the last decade, Germany seems to have reversed direction about the use of force.

In addition, the concept of normality only captures part of German foreign policy and therefore, even when used descriptively, can only be applied selectively. Those who describe the shift in German foreign policy in these terms tend to focus on Germany's pursuit of national interests and its selective multilateralism. However, if one defines normality by reference to France and the United Kingdom, it would seem to follow that Germany remains stubbornly and perhaps even increasingly "abnormal" in other aspects of foreign policy—especially security and defense policy. In the 1990s and in particular around the time of the Kosovo war in 1999, German security and defense policy looked to be converging with that of France and the United Kingdom as it reconciled itself to the use of military force as an instrument of foreign policy. In the last decade, however, Germany seems to have reversed direction. After September 11, Chancellor Schröder promised Germany's "unlimited solidarity" to the United States, committing troops to Operation Enduring Freedom and subsequently to the ISAF mission in Afghanistan. Germany still has around 5,000 troops in Afghanistan, although they are stationed mainly in the relatively peaceful north of the country and operate under strict caveats.

However, opposition to the mission in Afghanistan has gradually grown as German and civilian casualties have increased. Since 2007, opinion polls have consistently shown that a majority of Germans want their troops to be withdrawn from Afghanistan. A critical juncture came in September 2009, when a German colonel called in a U.S. air strike in Kunduz that killed dozens of civilians. The incident made many Germans realize that the *Bundeswehr* was fighting a war in Afghanistan rather than simply taking part in a "stabilization operation." In addition to the trauma of Afghanistan, the perceived failure of the Iraq war—which Germany opposed—has reinforced opposition to involvement of German troops in "out-of-area" operations. The abstention in the Security Council on Libya was a striking contrast to Germany's active involvement in the Kosovo war—a humanitarian intervention that did not even have a Security Council mandate.

To some extent, the German shift away from the use of military force is part of a Europe-wide trend: U.S. Secretary of Defense Robert Gates, for example, has spoken of the "demilitarization of Europe."[22] Nevertheless, even after making big defense cuts in 2010, France and the United Kingdom will continue to spend significantly more than Germany as a proportion of GDP, and still aim to project power in the world, as the treaties on defense cooperation they signed last November and the military intervention in Libya this year illustrate. Germany, on the other hand, is increasingly a consumer rather than a provider of security.[23] This "abnormality" is reflected in the way German politicians justify security-policy choices. For example, they defend Germany's refusal to deploy more troops in Afghanistan or lift the caveats under which they operate to support military intervention in Libya by using the language not of normality but of German exceptionalism. In matters of war and peace, it seems, Germans do not want to be "normal." In the end, therefore, the idea of normality is inadequate to capture the complex shift in the foreign policy of the Federal Republic since reunification.

Germany and "Geo-economics"

A different way of understanding the peculiarity of German power is through Edward Luttwak's concept of "geo-economics." In an essay in *The National*

Interest in 1990—almost exactly the same time that Maull was classifying Germany as a civilian power—Luttwak described how, in some parts of world, the role of military power was diminishing and "methods of commerce" were "displacing military methods"—"with disposable capital in lieu of firepower, civilian innovation in lieu of military–technical advancement, and market penetration in lieu of garrisons and bases."[24] In a way, he was describing a similar transformation as Maull. However, Luttwak argued that, although states were increasingly using one kind of *tool* rather than another, international relations would continue to follow the "logic of conflict," which was "adversarial, zero–sum, and paradoxical."[25] The neologism "geo-economics" was meant to capture this "admixture of the logic of conflict with the methods of commerce—or, as Clausewitz would have written, the logic of war in the grammar of commerce."[26]

The events of the next two decades seemed to disprove Luttwak's thesis of a shift from geopolitics to geo-economics. First the regional and ethnic conflicts of the 1990s and then 9/11 forced Western states to use military power. As we have seen, even states such as Germany that had for various reasons been reluctant to use military force came under increasing pressure to contribute to conflict resolution, not just financially but also in terms of troops on the ground. In fact, in the first decade of the post-Cold War world, it seemed as if conventional military power

> **G**ermany is applying the methods of commerce within a logic of conflict.

was more important than it had been previously, not less. However, subsequent developments—in particular the shift in the global distribution of power away from the United States toward rising powers such as China—seem to have vindicated Luttwak's argument. Two decades after he wrote the essay, his thesis seems to be a good way of explaining the actions of some states. It seems particularly apt given the apparent return of zero–sum competition between EU member states.

Like Maull, Luttwak was describing a general shift in the nature of power in international relations. However, he did not suggest that this shift would be universal or that it would take place everywhere at the same speed. It would not take place in "those unfortunate parts of the world where armed confrontations or civil strife persist for purely regional or internal reasons" and was most likely to take place where it was no longer possible to resort to military force, or as Luttwak put it, there was no "superior modality."[27] One could therefore particularly expect geo-economics—i.e., the methods of commerce—to play a greater role in the West, especially within the European Union. Luttwak also suggested that some states would be more "geo-economically active" than others: "The propensity of states to act geo-economically will vary greatly."[28]

The concept of geo-economics now seems particularly helpful as a way of describing the foreign policy of Germany, which has become more willing to impose its economic preferences on others within the European Union in the context of a discourse of zero–sum competition between the fiscally responsible and the fiscally irresponsible. For example, instead of accepting a moderate increase in inflation, which could harm the global competitiveness of its exports, Germany has insisted on austerity throughout the eurozone, even though this undermines the ability of states on the periphery to grow and threatens the overall cohesion of the European Union. In Luttwak's terms, Germany is applying the methods of commerce within a logic of conflict. In short, it may be helpful to understand Germany as a geo-economic power instead of (or perhaps as well as) a civilian power.

The nature of a geo-economic power is determined by the relationship between the state and business. As Luttwak acknowledges, "while states occupy virtually all of the world's political space, they occupy only a fraction of the total economic space."[29] He suggests that forms of co-existence between geo-economically active states and private economic actors will vary: it is intense in some cases and distant in others. Sometimes states "guide" large companies for their own geo-economic purposes and other times companies seek to manipulate politicians or bureaucracies. The relationship between the German state and

> Over the last decade, German exporters seem to have exerted greater influence on foreign policy.

business would seem to be an example of what Luttwak calls "reciprocal manipulation."[30] German companies lobby the German government to make policy that promotes their interests; they in turn help politicians maximize growth and in particular employment levels—the key measure of success in German politics.

This co-existence is particularly intense between the state—especially the economics ministry—and exporters, which have provided nearly half of German GDP and two-thirds of Germany's total GDP growth over the past decade. This disproportionate contribution of exports to growth means that German politicians are particularly dependent on exporters. However, because much of this growth has come from exports to economies such as China and Russia, where the state dominates business, exporters are also conversely dependent on the German government. As exports have increased as a share of GDP in the last decade, particularly since the Schröder government, German exporters seem to have exerted greater influence on German foreign policy. Thus German policy within the eurozone has increasingly focused on price stability at the expense of European integration as a political project. Meanwhile, German policy toward authoritarian states elsewhere in the world, such as China, has tended to focus on trade at the expense of human rights, democracy, and the rule of law.

Of course, Germany is not the only geo-economically active state in the world. Other states, such as China, also use geo-economic power. Indeed, there are striking parallels between China and Germany: both are manufacturer/exporters that have huge surpluses of saving over investment and have recently tended to impose deflationary pressures on their trading partners (the United States for China, the eurozone for Germany).[31] China, however, ultimately aspires to be a great power. Although it currently relies primarily on economic power in its rise, it is also committed to the use of military power.[32] (An influential concept among Chinese foreign-policy analysts is that of "comprehensive national power"—the idea that a successful foreign policy must be based on a "balanced power-profile" which includes military, political, and economic power.[33]) In that sense, Chinese foreign policy can be seen as a kind of neo-mercantilism. Germany, on the other hand, is unique in its combination of economic assertiveness and military abstinence. In a sense, therefore, it may be the purest example of a geo-economic power in the world today.

> The size of Germany's economy and interdependence is creating instability within Europe.

In the future, we can expect Germany to be increasingly willing to take decisions independently of—and sometimes in opposition to—its allies and partners, as it did during the Libya crisis. It is likely to pursue its national interests—defined above all else in economic terms—more assertively than it used to, while being more reluctant to transfer sovereignty to multilateral institutions. At the same time, however, it is likely to be reluctant to devote resources to solving international crises and in particular to use force, except where its economic interests are directly threatened. While the key aspiration of a civilian power is to civilize international relations, a geo-economic power is more likely to "hollow out" the international system.

The United States could, as a result, come into conflict with Germany in two ways. First, it could have disagreements about economic policy, as in last year's standoff between the two countries at the G-20 on issues such as stimulus spending and domestic demand. Secondly, it could struggle to persuade Germany to play an active role commensurate with its size and economic power on global security issues and on crisis management. Germany could be simply unwilling to provide resources, as in Afghanistan, or it could actively undermine initiatives led or supported by the United States, as in Libya. In this case, much will depend on Germany's role in the UN Security Council, where it has campaigned for a permanent seat since the Schröder government.

The Emergence of the German Geo-economic Question

From 1871 onwards, a unified Germany posed a problem for Europe. Its size and central location—the so-called *Mittellage*—meant that it was too powerful for a balance of power but not powerful enough to exercise hegemony. Germany created instability in Europe through its very existence. The "German question" appeared to have been resolved after World War II by the division of Germany and by the integration of the Federal Republic into the West through NATO and the European Union. With the transformation of Europe since the end of the Cold War, Germany has in a sense returned to the *Mittellage* in a geographic sense. However, whereas in the past Germany faced potential enemies on all sides and feared encirclement, it is now surrounded on all sides by NATO allies and EU partners. Germany's post-reunification "strategic saturation" and the interdependence of its economy with that of its neighbors in all directions means that it no longer seeks territorial expansion and no longer feels threatened. In geopolitical terms, Germany is benign.

However, the size of Germany's economy, and the interdependence between it and those around it, is now creating instability within Europe. After reunification, Germany became bigger, but was initially economically weaker as it struggled to deal with the costs of assimilating East Germany. Moreover, it saw its interests as being aligned with its NATO allies and EU partners. But during the last decade, as the German economy has recovered and a zero-sum discourse has returned within the European Union, Germany has become more willing to impose its preferences on others. Within the context of the European Union, Germany's economy is too big for any of its neighbors such as France to challenge (the "colossus" to which Habermas referred), but not big enough for Germany to exercise hegemony. In short, what appears to have happened is that the "German question" was resolved in geopolitical terms but has re-emerged in geo-economic form.

> The "German question" was resolved geopolitically, but has re-emerged in geo-economic form.

Notes

1. Sozialwissenschaftliches Institut der Bundeswehr, Sicherheits-und verteidigun-gspolitisches Meinungsklima in Deutschland. Ergebnisse der Bevölkerungsbefragung Oktober/November 2009, Kurzbericht, January 2010, pp. 33–37.

2. "'Politik zum Schieflachen': Interview mit Helmut Schmidt," *Cicero*, June 2010, http://www.cicero.de/97.php?ress_id=4&item=5147.

3. "L'Elysée s'abstient de critiquer Angela Merkel pour ne pas apparaître laxiste auprès des marches," *Le Monde*, March 19, 2010.

4. See for example Timothy Garton Ash, "Calling Germany, calling Germany: you alone can keep this eurozone show on the road," *The Guardian*, November 24, 2010, http://www.guardian.co.uk/commentisfree/2010/nov/24/germany-european-debt-euro-ireland.

5. Jürgen Habermas, "Germany's mindset has become solipsistic," *The Guardian*, June 11, 2010, http://www.guardian.co.uk/commentisfree/2010/jun/11/germany-normality-self-absorption.

6. Hanns W. Maull, "Germany and Japan: The New Civilian Powers," *Foreign Affairs* 69, no. 5 (Winter 1990/91), http://www.foreignaffairs.com/articles/46262/hanns-w-maull/germany-and-japan-the-new-civilian-powers.

7. Richard Rosecrance, *The Rise of the Trading State: Commerce and Conquest in the Modern World* (New York: Basic Books, 1986).

8. See for example Michael Staack, *Handelsstaat Deutschland. Deutsche Außenpolitik in einem neuen internationalen System* (Paderborn, 2000).

9. See Hanns W. Maull, "Zivilmacht Bundesrepublik Deutschland. Vierzehn Thesen für eine neue deutsche Außenpolitik," *Europa-Archiv* 47 (1992): pp. 269–278.

10. See Hanns W. Maull, "Germany and the Use of Force: Still a 'Civilian Power?'" *Survival* 42, no. 2 (Summer 2000): pp. 56–80; Hanns W. Maull, "Germany's foreign policy, post-Kosovo: Still a 'Civilian Power?'" in *Germany as a civilian power? The foreign policy of the Berlin Republic*, eds. Sebastian Harnisch and Hanns W. Maull (Manchester, 2001), pp. 108–127.

11. On "attritional" multilateralism, see Timothy Garton Ash, "Germany's Choice," *Foreign Affairs* 73, no. 4 (July/August 1994): p. 71.

12. For another interpretation of the shift away from reflexive multilateralism and its implications for Germany's attitude to the use of force, written before the euro and Libya crises, see Regina Karp, "The New German Foreign Policy Consensus," *The Washington Quarterly* 29, no. 1 (Winter 2005–06): pp. 61–82, http://www.twq.com/06winter/docs/06winter_karp.pdf.

13. Thomas Petersen, "Gemeinsames Interesse an Europa in Gefahr," Frankfurter Allgemeine Zeitung, January 25, 2011, http://www.faz.net/s/Rub99C3EECA60D84C0 8AD6B3E60C4EA807F/Doc ~EAE005CA324524217B16D205CA47FBE88 ~ATpl ~ Ecommon ~Scontent.html.

14. For the full text of the judgment, see http://www.bundesverfassungsgericht.de/entscheidungen/es20090630_2bve000208en.html.

15. Alexander Graf Lambsdorff, quoted in "Duell der Titanen," *Der Spiegel*, May 10, 2010.

16. Simon Tilford, "How to save the euro," Centre for European Reform, September 2010, p. 3, http://www.cer.org.uk/pdf/essay_euro_tilford_14sept10.pdf.

17. Ibid., p. 6.

18. George Soros, speech at Humboldt University, Berlin, June 23, 2010, http://www.georgesoros.com/interviews-speeches/entry/george_soros_speech_at_humboldt_university/.

19. See for example José-Ignacio Torreblanca, "Spain braces itself for a crisis made in Germany," *Financial Times*, November 29, 2010, http://www.ft.com/cms/s/0/bb515190-fbf2-11df-b7e9-00144feab49a.html#ixzz1FuTwGqF3.

20. On "zero-sum" competition in international relations since the economic crisis, see Gideon Rachman, *Zero-Sum World: Politics, Power and Prosperity after the Crash* (London, 2010).

21. See for example Timothy Garton Ash, "Berlin has cut the motor, but now Europe is stalled," *The Guardian*, March 31, 2010, http://www.guardian.co.uk/commentisfree/2010/mar/31/germany-europe-unity-self-interest. Garton Ash writes that "Germany has become a 'normal' nation, like France and Britain."

22. Robert Gates, speech at the National Defense University, Washington, D.C., February 23, 2010, http://www.defense.gov/speeches/speech.aspx?speechid=1423.

23. I am grateful to James Rogers for this point.

24. Edward Luttwak, "From geopolitics to geo-economics," *The National Interest*, Summer 1990, pp. 17–24. Reprinted in *The New Shape of World Politics* (New York: Norton, 1999), pp. 177–186. Here p. 177.

25. Ibid., p. 178.

26. Ibid., p. 180.

27. Ibid., p. 177.

28. Ibid., p. 184.

29. Ibid., p. 185.

30. Ibid.

31. See Martin Wolf, "China and Germany unite to impose global deflation," *Financial Times*, March 16, 2010, http://www.ft.com/cms/s/0/cd01f69e-3134-11df-8e6f-00144feabdc0.html.

32. Luttwak, "From geopolitics to geo-economics," *The New Shape of World Politics*, p. 183.

33. See Mark Leonard, *What Does China Think?* (London: PublicAffairs, 2008), pp. 84–86.

Brian Fishman

Al-Qaeda and the Rise of China: Jihadi Geopolitics in a Post-Hegemonic World

Prognosticating about China's economic, political, and military rise has become a favorite conversation for Western politicians and policy wonks. But Western observers are not the only strategists debating the impact of increased Chinese power. A parallel conversation has been taking place among al-Qaeda affiliated jihadi thinkers for much of the last decade. That discussion ranges from debate about how best to support rebellion among Muslim Uyghurs in China's Xinjiang province to more abstract disagreements over how a transnational militant network such as al-Qaeda should adapt when a traditional state upends the U.S.-led system that has been its primary boogeyman for nearly 15 years.

Although the Uyghur question tends to receive more attention, it is the latter issue that will be more important for both jihadi groups and China over the long run. China's growing economy and subsequent search for resources will increasingly tie it to regimes that al-Qaeda and its allies believe to be fundamentally corrupt, a fact that leaves jihadis conflicted about how to direct their energy today and questioning who will be their enemy tomorrow. Some jihadis enjoy the fact that the United States faces increased economic and political competition from China, but others argue that replacing the denomination of currency from dollars to yuan propping up hated Arab governments will not advance al-Qaeda's ultimate political and ideological goals. In the wake of Osama bin Laden's death, his successors are likely to reassess the global geopolitical picture and al-Qaeda's role in it. China will undoubtedly

Brian Fishman is a Counterterrorism Research Fellow at the New America Foundation and Research Fellow at the Combating Terrorism Center at West Point. He may be reached at Fishman@newamerica.net.

Copyright © 2011 Center for Strategic and International Studies
The Washington Quarterly • 34:3 pp. 47–62
DOI: 10.1080/0163660X.2011.588091

Al-Qaeda affiliated jihadi thinkers have been discussing China's rise for much of the last decade.

play a larger role in that conversation than it did when al-Qaeda was founded in 1988 or when the group focused its energy squarely on the United States in 1998. Indeed, al-Qaeda and its adherents will likely shift some of their focus away from the United States as the geopolitical playing field levels, but those jihadis are more likely to focus on attacking local regimes before embracing the Sino-centric analysis of the jihadi movement's most farsighted strategic analysts.

As al-Qaeda wrestles with an old-fashioned shift in the global distribution of state power, China must determine how to evolve its traditional foreign policy memes in response to the transnational problems posed by al-Qaeda and its allies. China's traditional policy of non-intervention in the internal affairs of other countries has served it reasonably well for 60 years and continues to create certain advantages in negotiations with less-than-humanitarian regimes in the Middle East and Africa. But sub-national and transnational threats will challenge the doctrine of non-interventionism, which is grounded in a decidedly Westphalian understanding of the world. China has already grown somewhat more forward-leaning in dealing with some transnational threats, including pirates off of East Africa, but jihadi groups represent a challenge that is both broader and potentially more disruptive. To date, China has responded to a potential threat from al-Qaeda by minimizing rhetorical confrontation and hoping that al-Qaeda's operators remain focused elsewhere. But 10 years after 9/11, global jihadis such as al-Qaeda view China's economic and political support for "apostate" regimes a terrible offense. That, coupled with the increasing prominence of the Uyghurs in jihadi propaganda, suggests China will not be able to avoid al-Qaeda forever.

Jihadi Strategic Thinking about China

Osama bin Laden and al-Qaeda have been singularly focused on attacking the United States as a way to produce revolution in the Middle East since 1998, and paid relatively little attention to China during the period of Taliban rule in Afghanistan. That is not to say that China did not have a problem with militants during that period. Like Islamic revolutionaries around the globe, Uyghur groups committed to revolution in China's Xinjiang province established camps alongside al-Qaeda in Taliban-ruled Afghanistan. But despite their freedom to train in Afghanistan, the Taliban banned fighters from the East Turkestan Islamic Movement (ETIM) from attacking China from their territory.

The Taliban's prohibition on attacking China reflected its inherent caution about attacks on great powers (a prudence that extended to the United States) but also reflected its broader geopolitical analysis of China's role in the international system. In his opus, *The Call to Global Islamic Resistance*, the prominent jihadi strategist Abu Mus'ab al-Suri explained Taliban policy toward ETIM and China during the 1990s:

> China's growing economy will increasingly tie it to regimes that al-Qaeda believes are corrupt.

> The jihadists of Eastern Turkistan went back to their homeland and recruited mujahidin who were brought back to Afghanistan and trained in military tactics, which were to be used against the Chinese government... This group recognized Mullah Omar as the official imam. Facing strong American pressure, the Taliban ordered the East Turkistan group to cease their attacks against China. The Taliban wanted friendly relations with China as a way to counter the American threat.[1]

Although the Taliban ordered Osama bin Laden not to attack the United States, they did accept his assessment that the United States was a central threat to the Taliban regime and, according to al-Suri, established a foreign policy that responded to that threat. Bin Laden ultimately ignored Mullah Omar's admonition not to attack the United States, but he followed the Taliban's China policy closely.[2] Bin Laden even referred to China publicly to bolster his case that the United States was an illegitimate and aggressive hegemon, accusing the United States of preventing Beijing's rise to global prominence rather than offering support to the largely-Muslim Uyghurs. In 1997, after a series of bombings in Beijing that most ascribed to Uyghur separatists, bin Laden blamed the CIA, saying, "The United States wants to incite conflict between China and the Muslims. The Muslims of Xinjiang are being blamed for the bomb blasts in Beijing. But I think these explosions were sponsored by the American CIA. If Afghanistan, Pakistan, Iran and China get united, the United States and India will become ineffective."[3]

Bin Laden was so intent on ascribing evil to the United States that he disregarded information about a Uyghur rebellion and explained that China was really a natural enemy of the United States:

> I often hear about Chinese Muslims, but since we have no direct connection with people in China and no member of our organization comes from China, I don't have any detailed knowledge about them. The Chinese government is not fully aware of the intentions of the United States and Israel. These two countries also want to usurp the resources of China... So I suggest the Chinese government be more careful of the U.S. and the West.[4]

> Transnational threats will challenge the Chinese doctrine of non-intervention in others' internal affairs.

Perhaps to the frustration of Uyghur activists at the time, the Taliban and al-Qaeda both sought to avoid conflict with China, a point that the ETIM amir, Hassan Mahsum, made in a 2002 interview with *Radio Free Asia*.[5] True or not, according to Mahsum, ETIM had "absolutely no relationship with Usama Bin Ladin, and we have never received any help from him. All our activities are entirely directed at liberating East Turkistan territory from Chinese invaders, to drive the Chinese invaders out of that land."[6]

Although circumstances have changed tremendously, the strategic questions facing the Taliban and al-Qaeda regarding China in the late 1990s presaged contemporary jihadi disagreements over how to deal with China. Whereas some jihadis today view growing Chinese political and economic strength as an opportunity to weaken the United States, others view it as another infidel power that will persecute Muslims by using economic support to prop up regimes that jihadis aim to destroy.

Even after 9/11, al-Suri debated with himself about the appropriate jihadi policy toward China. He dabbled with the idea that China could be attracted as an ally in a war focused on the United States, but concluded that was only possible if jihadi movements could achieve a degree of international legitimacy and "escape this terrorist accusation."[7] Al-Suri recognized that geopolitical tension was likely to grow between the United States and China, but worried that if the jihadis were to "overcome America" then "in all likelihood [China] will conspire against us at the appropriate time and circumstances."[8]

Some jihadis have since disagreed with al-Suri's conclusion that China was likely to be an enemy over the long run. Hamid al-Ali, a prominent Kuwaiti activist and religious adviser well known among jihadis around the globe, has argued that competition between the United States and China for allies and resources creates opportunities for jihadis to reduce U.S. global influence, which he said was the heart of the al-Qaeda project. In a series of essays written from late 2007 through 2008, al-Ali developed the idea that patterns of global power were shifting and brought a "return to the Cold War" that jihadis should aim to exploit.[9] In the post-9/11 world, al-Ali argued, the United States had been weakened because its economy and military had been over-extended, while China, Iran, and Russia were strengthened as a result.[10]

With the important exception of increased Iranian power, which he disavowed because of the Iranian regime's Shia theology, al-Ali deemed these developments positive and argued that Arab regimes in particular were missing an opportunity "to get rid of the slavery to American imperialism."[11] Echoing a host of Western analysts, al-Ali interpreted China's increased political and economic prominence in Africa as a major setback for U.S. goals in the region because it offered governments the ability to ignore U.S. demands about governance. Increasing Arab relations with China, he argued, would produce a similar result, "with the biggest loser being the Zionists."[12]

Putting aside al-Ali's ignorance of the relatively constructive relations between Israel and China, his argument is important because of the way he conceptualized jihadi victory over the United States.[13] Maintaining bin Laden's focus on the United States as puppet master for corrupt regimes in the Middle East, al-Ali imagines victory over the United States resulting from geopolitical power shifts, not just jihadi war. It would be a win for al-Qaeda, he argued, to facilitate global power shifts headlined by China so that the U.S. relationship with Arab governments in the Middle East is less cooperative. Implicit in al-Ali's argument is the idea that at least some Arab regimes are salvageable, and that certain sources of external support for such regimes are not objectionable. For him, the jihadis' real problem is the United States.

Al-Ali's analysis is striking because it is so traditional. This global jihadi, a champion of Internet communications who seems the very embodiment of a 21st-century transnational threat, sees opportunity in decidedly 20th- (or even 19th-) century geopolitical analysis. What's good for China is bad for the United States. And what is bad for the United States is good for jihadis.

> Some argue what is bad for the U.S. is good for jihadis; others think that's too narrow a focus on the U.S.

Other jihadis argue that such an approach reflects too narrow a focus on the United States as the root of global infidelity. Akram Hijazi, a Jordanian professor who has become a major intellectual figure for jihadi strategists, wrote a three-part assessment of China in mid-2007 that concluded China may replace the United States as the world's dominant economic and military force, but that in the process of doing so, it will simply take the place of the United States as the "head of the snake."[14]

Hijazi argued that the United States is indeed in decline as a result of increasing Chinese economic competition (an assertion he backed with an impressive array of statistics) but fretted that an ascendant China would not actually improve the position of jihadi groups. In May 2010, citing agreements between China and Israel as well as China's suppression of Uyghur riots, he concluded that such concerns were justified, and went on to mourn a weak Arab response to China's crackdown on the Uyghurs. Using sarcasm to echo the typical jihadi critique of Arab governments responding to perceived offensives from the United States, Hijazi lamented that:

> [China] committed no wrong against Muslims except for being a brutal and colonizing power... It has committed no wrong against humanity except for being a deceiving country... [that] drained the resources of the weak countries. As for the real culprits, it is us, Arabs and Muslims who no more have dignity and honor. It is us who bet on miserable ideological stances through which we forget ourselves for decades and decades.[15]

Not surprisingly, Hijazi's arguments have been collected and redistributed by jihadi propagandists highlighting the Uyghur cause. Since 2008, a new and decidedly more jihadi brand of Uyghur activism has begun to draw on global jihadi networks to publicize its cause, and in doing so may increase the likelihood of conflict between jihadi groups and China. The ETIM went quiet in 2003 after Mahsum, its amir, was killed by Pakistani forces. But in early 2008, a new group calling itself the Turkistan Islamic Party (TIP) announced itself as ETIM's successor and began distributing propaganda that was increasingly religious, produced in Arabic and distributed on Arabic-language jihadi forums.[16] The TIP made a series of threats to the Beijing Olympics, and in July 2008 released a video claiming responsibility for bus bombings in Shanghai and China's Yunnan Province.[17] Six months later, the TIP's propaganda began to be released through the al-Fajr Media Center, a clearinghouse for jihadi media that distributes propaganda for al-Qaeda central and several affiliates.[18]

But the Uyghur cause did not hit the jihadi mainstream until July 2009 when the Chinese government violently suppressed riots in Xinjiang between Uyghurs and Han Chinese. In the wake of those clashes, the amir of the TIP, Abd-al-Haqq Turkistani, called for violence not just inside China but against Chinese interests around the globe. Speaking in Uyghur, but accompanied by an Arabic transcript, Turkistani said, "The Chinese must be targeted inside and outside the country. Their embassies, consulates, headquarters and gatherings must be targeted, and their men and families must be killed to redeem our brothers who are detained in East Turkistan. All these acts are a support to our brothers in East Turkistan."[19]

At least some of Turkistani's audience was eager to hear his message. Two weeks beforehand, al-Qaeda in the Islamic Maghreb (AQIM) threatened to respond to the violence in Xinjiang by attacking Chinese interests in Algeria.[20] In classic al-Qaeda fashion, China's local insurrection was being linked to global events and used to promote violent activism around the world. In October 2009, the senior jihadi ideologue Abu Yahya al-Libi urged solidarity with the Uyghurs and compared China's policy in Xinjiang to Israeli policy in the West Bank, but notably stopped short of calling for violence against Chinese interests globally.[21] He also refrained from explicitly supporting the TIP as an organization.[22]

Even as Arab elements of al-Qaeda have increased their focus on militancy in Xinjiang, a group reportedly tied to the TIP has dabbled in operations outside of China and expanded its list of targets beyond Chinese infrastructure. In July 2010, three men linked to the TIP were arrested in Norway and accused of plotting to attack the Chinese embassy there as well as offices of the *Jyllands Posten* newspaper, which in 2005 had published cartoons of the Prophet Muhammad.[23] If those accusations are accurate, the plot reflects a synthesis of jihadi global ideological concepts and more traditional insurrection against China.[24] For all the debate among jihadis about whether the rise of China is good or bad, the trend line of jihadi thinking is clear: it leads toward confrontation with the Chinese state.

> The trend line of jihadi thinking is clear: it leads toward confrontation with the Chinese state.

Chinese Strategy toward Global Jihadis

Chinese security policy was not upended like the United States' on 9/11, but it has evolved as a result of both non-state militants and the behavioral shifts they have prompted from the United States and other Western powers. Although the most important impact of 9/11 for Chinese security policy was to bring U.S. troops into Central Asia in large numbers, the global focus on al-Qaeda offered China the opportunity to justify its suppression of Uyghur political and separatist movements in Xinjiang.[25]

China's initial strategy was, rather predictably, to focus on acquiring international support for its efforts to maintain domestic stability, which it did by accepting U.S. intervention in Afghanistan (which shares a very short border with China) while linking Uyghur separatists to al-Qaeda in order to pressure the United States to label such groups as terrorist organizations. The United States ultimately labeled ETIM a terrorist organization, but did not designate other groups as such.

But Beijing's calculation to link its domestic security challenges to the global jihadi threat has grown far more complex in the decade since 9/11. China's economic interests have grown exponentially around the world, including with regimes that jihadis aim to overthrow, and at least some Uyghurs have embraced the linkage to jihadi groups. Those shifts have, for the first time, raised the possibility that ideologically-motivated jihadis far from China will be compelled to attack Chinese interests in much the same way that they have the United States. In response, China has begun to revert to its pre-9/11 tendency of downplaying the threat from Uyghur groups such as the jihadi-linked TIP and generally framing such groups as an internal problem disconnected from al-Qaeda.

Modern Uyghur rebellion against Chinese rule in Xinjiang goes back to at least 1962, when tens of thousands of Uyghurs fled Xinjiang for the Soviet Kazakh Republic.[26] As the Sino–Soviet split deepened, some of these émigrés even appealed to Moscow for assistance, which responded by supporting the exiles and sponsoring Uyghur-language propaganda in Central Asia.[27] But China successfully countered the internationalization of its domestic security problem. The Soviets ultimately did little to support Uyghur nationalism (likely because of concerns it could spur separatism in their own Central Asian territories) despite appeals from Uyghur groups as late as 1990.[28] The fact that Uyghur groups appealed to the Soviet Union illustrates how far outside the jihadi mainstream Uyghur groups were in 1990—appealing for help from the failing superpower that had just been defeated in Afghanistan by local mujahideen and a global coalition of Muslim fighters drawn by the religious imperative of resisting an infidel invader.

Following the Soviet collapse, China's burgeoning political and economic power was a compelling reason for the new Central Asian states to avoid supporting the Uyghur groups. When the Shanghai Cooperation Organization (SCO) was formed in 1996 (the original members were China, Kazakhstan, Kyrgyzstan, and Tajikistan; Uzbekistan became a member in 2001), the Tajiks, Uzbeks, and Kazakhs all increased pressure on Uyghur organizations to reduce separatist activism.[29] China's appeal to these and other states, including those in the Middle East and Africa, has been to dramatically increase economic ties and to remove the domestic political issues of either state from discussion.

Jihadi thinkers like Akram Hijazi complain that Arab and Muslim states have not supported Muslim Uyghur separatists, and indeed, China has rarely demonstrated concern that foreign Islamic militants would support Uyghur separatists. Like the United States, China gave aid and weapons to Afghan mujahideen fighting Soviet forces in Afghanistan during the 1980s, and it built strong ties with Pakistan even as the Pakistani state supported the Taliban's rise in Kabul during the mid-1990s.[30] China's support for Pakistan and Pakistan's support for the Taliban paid some dividends for Beijing—China became the first non-Islamic country to gain an ambassadorial meeting with Mullah Omar in 2000.[31] Like the authorities in other Central Asian states, Mullah Omar assured the ambassador that he had no desire to interfere in Chinese affairs and would not allow "any group to use its territory to conduct any such operations."[32]

China, which was never close to the Taliban regime, distanced itself further after 9/11, falling back on the idea of non-intervention in the affairs of other countries, explaining that it would "never interfere in Afghanistan's internal affairs."[33] But shortly thereafter, China began to reframe its internal struggle with Uyghur groups for a global audience newly energized to confront terrorist groups. During the 1990s, Chinese official media referred to Uyghur nationalist movements as "splittists" (*fenliezhuryizhe*), but in the years following 9/11 increasingly referred to them as "terrorists" (*kongbufenzi*).[34] The shift in terminology was codified in a January 2002 white paper "opposing the application of double standards concerning the anti-terrorism issue" and calling for an international crackdown on Uyghur groups as part of the broader war on terrorism.[35] In contrast to earlier Chinese efforts to downplay Uyghur violence in Xinjiang, the document included a long list of supposed terrorist attacks and argued that ETIM had been directly trained by bin Laden's forces in Afghanistan.[36]

The precise extent of links between al-Qaeda and ETIM prior to 9/11 remains unclear, but the shift in China's framing of the Uyghur issue following 9/11 is not. And from China's perspective, the shift in tone helped garner international acquiescence for its efforts to suppress Uyghur separatism. On August 19, 2002, the U.S. State Department designated ETIM as an official terrorist organization and subsequently petitioned the United Nations to add the group to its list of terrorist organizations, which it did on September 11, 2002.[37] Although China did not get everything that it wanted from these designations (Uyghur groups that had not had a presence in Afghanistan under the Taliban regime were not listed), the U.S. and UN actions offered public validation of Chinese policy.[38]

International designation of ETIM as a terrorist organization has not meant that all Uyghurs in Afghanistan have been treated as jihadi-linked militants. A number of Uyghur activists in Afghanistan captured and imprisoned in Guantanamo were found to have little relation to al-Qaeda. Some of those activists have nonetheless found themselves in political and legal limbo.[39] The United States has slowly released Uyghur detainees to third countries rather than repatriate them to China, which has prompted China to accuse the United States of maintaining a double-standard regarding terrorism.[40]

But if China has not been able to compel the United States to turn over Uyghur activists, it has generally succeeded at deflecting global attention from crackdowns on Uyghur groups in China itself. As noted by Akram Hijazi, even Arab and Muslim states have generally sidestepped the issue, even as it grew more prominent in 2009 when the major riots in Xinjiang between Uyghurs and Han Chinese provoked a widespread security crackdown. The explanation seems to be the growing Chinese economic relationships with a wide range of countries, but especially those in the Mideast and Africa. Trade between China and the Arab world leaped from $36.4 billion in 2004 to $107.4 billion in 2010,[41] while Chinese trade with African countries erupted over the last decade, rising tenfold to more than $100 billion in 2010.[42]

The silence from Muslim governments is grounded in growing economic relations but it is also bolstered by China's policy of non-intervention in the internal affairs of its trading partners.[43] Indeed the policy of non-intervention that was praised by jihadi thinker Hamid al-Ali has meant that Muslim governments are less disposed to confront China on its internal challenges.[44] China remains relatively popular among Arab populations, not just its governing elite. A 2010 poll found that China (16 percent) is second only to France (35 percent) among Arabs when asked which country they would prefer to be the world's only superpower. When asked which two countries posed the biggest threat to them, only three percent answered China compared to 77 percent that mentioned the United States (Israel ranked highest with 88 percent).[45]

But if China came through the 2009 riots relatively unscathed diplomatically (the only strong protest to Chinese action in the Muslim world came from Turkey, which shares historical and linguistic ties with the Uyghurs), the incident illustrated the limitations and risks to China of a policy linking the internal Uyghur threat to global militant movements.[46] Linking Uyghur activism to al-Qaeda or similar movements implicitly draws attention to these groups' commonalities and might highlight aspects of the Uyghur rebellion that could garner wider sympathy among populations in the Middle East and Africa.

The further challenge for China is that linking Uyghur activism to global jihadis risks globalizing the Uyghur separatist movement into a cause célèbre for jihadi supporters everywhere. As China's international economic interests grow, the danger posed by jihadi activism to critical Chinese economic infrastructure outside its borders has grown substantially. The acquisition of raw materials from abroad is now a critical element of China's economic strategy, which in turn is fundamental to domestic stability. Even considering the intensity of Uyghur–Han rioting in Xinjiang in 2009, such upheavals are occurring on China's periphery and are controllable by China's increasingly competent domestic security forces.

China's economic growth is not just critical for its existing regime. China is increasingly a critical economic partner for governments around the world, including many that jihadi groups linked to al-Qaeda consider worthy of overthrowing. For example, in response to international pressure to decrease imports from Iran, China has steadily increased oil imports from Saudi Arabia.[47] In 2009, China imported nearly as much oil from Saudi Arabia as the United States did (839,000 barrels/day to 980,000 barrels/day) and relied on Saudi Arabia for a much larger percentage of its overall imports (20.5 percent compared to 8.5 percent).[48] Such numbers may be somewhat anomalous as a result of China's short-term efforts to apply pressure on Iran by resourcing oil imports, but they nonetheless illustrate a shift in global demand that will increasingly make China a key economic powerhouse providing economic support to regimes that are the ultimate target of al-Qaeda's ire.[49]

That al-Qaeda aims to target Western economic interests as a means of severing Arab and Muslim regimes from their foreign suitors is well-known, but the strategy begs the question of whether that energy will be redirected toward Chinese interests as it becomes an increasingly important market for Middle Eastern governments. AQIM's threat to attack Chinese workers in Algeria, where China has important energy interests, suggests that it will at some point.[50]

Such threats are not likely to substantially change China's approach to domestic, "separatist, terrorist, or extremist" groups, but they may impact China's diplomatic and rhetorical approach. With the exception of specific forums where raising the specter of terrorism remains useful, such as the United Nations or in bilateral talks with the United States, China is less likely to link its domestic challenges in Xinjiang with jihadist groups like al-Qaeda. Such connections proved useful in the wake of 9/11, but international approval or disapproval has not appreciably changed China's ability or willingness to use force in Xinjiang. Linking China's confrontation with the Uyghurs to jihadis does have a definite downside however, drawing jihadi attention to the issue which increasingly carries the potential to threaten China's ever more far-flung economic empire.

Of course, not all of that empire is so far-flung. China has invested seriously in Pakistan and cultivated the state as an ally against the more pressing geopolitical threat of India.[51] It has also invested substantially in Afghanistan's mineral deposits, including a $3.2 billion investment in the Aynak copper mine. Such commitments inevitably invest China in the stability of both countries, though China may be heartened by its long and deep relations with the Pakistani military and intelligence establishment, which still has important influence over militant groups in the region.[52] Nonetheless, al-Qaeda and other militants in the region have grown increasingly opposed to the Pakistani state, and they may perceive Chinese support for it as illegitimate and worthy of disrupting. That has had repercussions for Chinese interests in Pakistan, including the kidnapping of Chinese engineers in the country and attacks on Chinese masseuses prior to the 2007 Red Mosque incident.[53] Like the rest of the world, China must come to terms with a Pakistan that cannot control the militants it helped create.

> **M**ilitants may perceive Chinese support for the Pakistani state as illegitimate and worthy of disrupting.

Geostrategic Implications

The evolving relationship between jihadis and China has implications for the United States. Since 1998, al-Qaeda has justified its existence on the grounds of a particular geopolitical circumstance: one in which U.S. economic and military power has been supreme globally and has provided critical backing for Arab regimes. Those conditions have now changed and, like other actors evolving to deal with new geopolitical realities, al-Qaeda will as well. China's increased economic, military, and political power will create tension with the United States in many areas, but it also will create opportunities for cooperation.

It will not be easy, however, for the United States to utilize these developments to generate greater cooperation with the Chinese. The threat from jihadi groups to China—no matter their intentions—is simply not large enough to dramatically change Beijing's outlook in the short run, and China knows that it can continue to rely on U.S. efforts to suppress al-Qaeda's most virulent elements and secure the global commons. Indeed, China is likely to be most aggressive supporting security forces and bolstering stability where the United States has the least presence—in Africa and parts of the Middle East. China will accept the costs of global leadership only when the United States will not.

Al-Qaeda, meanwhile, has a minimal ability to attack China directly and it is unlikely to redirect substantial resources to support jihadi-leaning Uyghur factions in the near term. Al-Qaeda has long willingly ignored the Uyghur separatist movement in China, and it is hard to escape the conclusion that is in part a response to a core geopolitical analysis and unwillingness to anger both the United States and China simultaneously. It is no wonder that jihadis have championed the Uyghur cause more loudly as the relationship between al-Qaeda and former Taliban rulers in Kabul has frayed.

Certainly, coordinated U.S. and Chinese pressure on the Pakistani intelligence establishment could make al-Qaeda and its allies more insecure. More likely are attacks against Chinese economic and diplomatic targets farther afield in areas where Chinese economic and political support is particularly important for the local regime, especially in North Africa where Chinese infrastructure is increasingly prominent. Jihadi-supported attacks on Chinese interests in Southeast Asia are possible as well, and could be designed to exploit existing ethnic tension involving ethnic Chinese populations on the Malay Peninsula or in Indonesia. Jihadi pressure on Chinese interests in Pakistan is also possible, but most likely from relatively marginalized groups trying to differentiate themselves and provoke interest from the Pakistani state, which values its relationship with China highly.

In spite of the arguments of Hamid al-Ali and others that Chinese investment is less onerous than U.S. engagement with Arab or Muslim governments, jihadis are likely to view China as an enemy in the coming years. Al-Qaeda will quietly cheer competition between the United States and China, and is unlikely to redirect resources to attack China in the short run, but it also is unlikely to embrace Chinese influence in the Muslim world if Beijing tacitly supports existing governments. Nonetheless, al-Qaeda's ideological dogmatism has taken on a life of its own—and much of that vitriol is framed around opposition to the United States specifically. Even if intellectual leaders of the al-Qaeda movement shift their geostrategic analysis, the more visceral ideas motivating operational cells are likely to change more slowly.

Al-Qaeda after Osama bin Laden is likely to lose some of its global perspective and refocus on targeting local regimes for jihadi revolution. Although bin Laden was uniquely obsessed with the United States, his successors are more likely to focus their energy on vulnerable local regimes rather than the "next" superpower. Bin Laden, after all, has been the symbol of jihadi unity since 9/11, but that coalition is an inherently fractious one. In the near term, a confrontation with China is more likely to stem from jihadi activism in a state where China has built and utilizes critical infrastructure than from a concerted global strategy to identify and target Chinese interests specifically.

Finally for Beijing, al-Qaeda's reaction is but one factor that may force China to reconsider its longstanding policy of non-interference in the affairs of other states. To jihadi enemies of various Arab and Muslim autocracies, economic investment and political support for a leading clique constitutes meddling and may provoke a violent backlash. Although non-intervention is cited by some jihadis as a reason why China would be a better partner for various governments than the United States, the larger lesson of al-Qaeda's global prominence is that strategic concepts based on the immutability of nation–states and unchallenged authority of governments are increasingly suspect. Even if the Uyghur issue does not bring China into conflict with jihadi groups, Beijing's role in economically sustaining targeted governments ultimately will.

Notes

1. Abu Mus'ab al-Suri, *The Call to Global Islamic Resistance*, p. 727.
2. Al-Suri's general assessment of the Taliban's reasoning was echoed by Abdul Salam Zaeef, the Taliban ambassador to Pakistan before 9/11. See Abdul Salam Zaeef, *My Life With the Taliban*, eds. Alex Strick van Linschoten and Felix Kuehn (New York: Columbia University Press, 2010), p. 135.
3. Hamid Mir, "Interview with Usama bin Laden," *Pakistan*, March 18, 1997.
4. Abu Shiraz, "May 1998 Interview with Bin Laden," *Pakistan*, February 20, 1999. See also Rahimullah Yusufzai, "In the Way of Allah," *The News*, June 15, 1998.
5. Interview with Hassan Mahsum, *Radio Free Asia*, January 22, 2002.

6. Ibid.

7. Al-Suri, p. 1113.

8. Ibid., p. 714.

9. Hamid al-Ali, "Return to the Cold War," October 19, 2007, www.h-alali.com.

10. Hamid al-Ali, "Post 9/11 World," Ana al-Muslim, September 11, 2008.

11. Hamid al-Ali, "What is Behind the Growth of China?" March 21, 2008, www.h-alali.com.

12. Ibid.

13. Degang Sun, "China and the Global Jihad Network," The Journal of the Middle East and Africa 1, no. 2, pp. 196–207.

14. Akram Hijazi, "China Under the Microscope of the Salafi Jihad," August 15, 2007, www.drakramhijazi.maktooblog.com.

15. Akram Hijazi, "Chinese Slaps," Tahadi Islamic Network, May 18, 2010.

16. Kirk Sowell, "Promoting Jihad Against China: The Turkistani Islamic Party in Arabic Jihadist Media," An Independent Report Commissioned by Sky News, August 1, 2010, http://www.kirksowell.com/Content/Documents/TIP%20Special%20Report.pdf.

17. "Our Blessed Jihad," Turkistan Islamic Party Voice of Islam Information Center, July 23, 2008.

18. "Turkistan Islamic Party Statement," released by al-Fajr Media Center, February 26, 2009.

19. Abd-al-Haqq Turkistani, "China's Massacres and Barbarism Will Not Go Unpunished," al-Fajr Media Center, July 31, 2009.

20. Chris Zambelis, "Uighur Dissent and Militancy in China's Xinjiang Province," CTC Sentinel 3, no. 1 (January 2010).

21. Abu Yahya al-Libi, "East Turkistan: The Forgotten Wound," As-Sahab Media Center, October 6, 2009.

22. Sowell, "Promoting Jihad Against China."

23. Edward Wong, "Chinese Separatists Tied to Norway Bomb," The New York Times, July 9, 2010, http://www.nytimes.com/2010/07/10/world/asia/10uighur.html; Walter Gibbs and John Acher, "Suspects Admit Bomb Plots in Denmark, Norway: Police," Reuters, September 28, 2010, http://af.reuters.com/article/worldNews/idAFTRE68R5AR20100928.

24. For more discussion of these trends, see: Thomas Hegghammer, "The Ideological Hybridization of Jihadi Groups," Current Trends in Islamist Ideology, vol. 9, November 18, 2009, http://www.currenttrends.org/research/detail/the-ideological-hybridization-of-jihadi-groups.

25. For an excellent discussion of Chinese policy in South Asia since 2001, see Andrew Small, "China's Caution on Afghanistan-Pakistan," The Washington Quarterly 33, no. 3 (July 2010): pp. 81-97, http://twq.com/10july/docs/10jul_Small.pdf.

26. Gardner Bovingdon, The Uyghurs: Strangers in their Own Land (New York: Columbia University Press, 2010), p. 141.

27. Ibid., p. 143.

28. Ibid., p. 143.

29. Ibid., p. 145.

30. Steve Coll, Ghost Wars (New York: Penguin Books, 2004), p. 66; Small, "China's Caution on Afghanistan-Pakistan."

31. At the meeting, Mullah Omar reportedly assured the Chinese ambassador that ETIM would not be allowed to attack China from Afghanistan. See: Syed Saleem Shahzad, "Secrets of the Taliban's Success," The Asia Times, September 11, 2008, http://www.atimes.com/atimes/South_Asia/JI11Df01.html.

32. Zaeef, p. 135.
33. "Chinese Foreign Ministry Spokesperson on the Reported Relations Between China and Taliban," September 15, 2001, http://www.china-un.org/eng/chinaandun/securitycouncil/thematicissues/counterterrorism/t26904.htm.
34. Arienne M. Dwyer, "The Xinjiang Conflict: Uyghur Identity, Language Policy, and Political Discourse," East-West Center Washington, Policy Studies 15 (2005), http://www.eastwestcenter.org/fileadmin/stored/pdfs/PS015.pdf; Chinese officials often use the construction of the "three evils," meaning "terrorism, separatism, and extremism."
35. Information Office of the State Council, "'East Turkistan' Terrorist Forces Cannot Get Away with Impunity," Xinhua, January 21, 2002, http://news.xinhuanet.com/english/2002-01/21/content_247082.htm.
36. Ibid.
37. For designation, see Shirley A. Kan, "U.S.-China Counterterrorism Cooperation: Issues for U.S. Policy," CRS Report for Congress, renowned RL33001, updated September 11, 2008, http://fpc.state.gov/documents/organization/110764.pdf; "Press Statement on the UN Designation of the Eastern Turkistan Islamic Movement," U.S. Department of the Treasury Press Release, September 12, 2002.
38. Bovingdon, pp. 135–136.
39. Warren Richey, "Innocent, but in limbo at Guantanamo," The Christian Science Monitor, February 13, 2006, http://www.csmonitor.com/2006/0213/p03s03-usju.html.
40. Anthony Kuhn, "U.S., China Debate Over Uighur Guantanamo Detainees," NPR, February 20, 2009, http://www.npr.org/templates/story/story.php?storyId=100790460.
41. "Chinese Premier Urges Upgrading China-Arab Cooperation," Xinhua, May 14, 2010, http://news.xinhuanet.com/english2010/china/2010-05/14/c_13293384.htm.
42. William Wallis and Tom Burgis, "Continent Drives a Harder Bargain," Financial Times, June 14, 2010, http://www.ft.com/cms/s/0/85632536-74ed-11df-aed7-00144feabdc0.html.
43. See Abigail Hauslohner, "In the Middle East, Little Outcry Over China's Uighurs," Time, July 17, 2009, http://www.time.com/time/world/article/0,8599,1911002,00.html.
44. For more on Arab and Chinese ties, see Chris Zambelis and Brandon Gentry, "China through Arab Eyes: American Influence in the Middle East," Parameters 38, no. 1 (Spring 2008): pp. 60–72.
45. Shibley Telhami, "2010 Arab Public Opinion Poll," Brookings Institute, August 5, 2010, http://www.brookings.edu/~/media/Files/rc/reports/2010/08_arab_opinion_poll_telhami/08_arab_opinion_poll_telhami.pdf.
46. For more on Chinese relations with the Arab world and the impact of China's conflict with the Uyghurs, see Charles Horner and Eric Brown, "Beijing's Islamic Complex," The American Interest, May-June 2010, http://www.the-american-interest.com/article-bd.cfm?piece=805.
47. Rowena Mason, "How the U.S. Aims to Reduce Iran's Oil-Barter Power," The Daily Telegraph, December 6, 2010, http://www.telegraph.co.uk/finance/newsbysector/energy/oilandgas/8182532/How-the-US-aims-to-reduce-Irans-oil-barter-power.html.
48. For U.S. numbers, see http://www.eia.doe.gov/dnav/pet/pet_move_impus_d_nus_NSA_mbblpd_a.htm. For Chinese numbers, see http://www.eia.doe.gov/cabs/china/pdf.pdf.
49. Jad Mouawad, "China's Growth Shifts the Geopolitics of Oil," The New York Times, March 19, 2010, http://www.nytimes.com/2010/03/20/business/energy-environment/20saudi.html.
50. Jane Macartney, "Al-Qaeda Vows Revenge on China After Riots," The Times, July 15, 2009, http://www.timesonline.co.uk/tol/news/world/asia/article6704812.ece.

51. Small, "China's Caution on Afghanistan-Pakistan."
52. "Mullen: Pakistan's ISI Spy Agency has 'Militant Links'," *BBC News*, April 21, 2011, http://www.bbc.co.uk/news/world-south-asia-13153538.
53. Small, "China's Caution on Afghanistan-Pakistan."

Michael Fullilove

China and the United Nations: The Stakeholder Spectrum

In December 2009, representatives of 192 nations—not to mention thousands of journalists, activists, and business executives—assembled in Copenhagen for the 15th Conference of the Parties to the United Nations Framework Convention on Climate Change (UNFCCC). The goal was to strike a new international agreement to replace the Kyoto Protocol, due to expire in 2012—one that would lead to meaningful reductions of greenhouse gas emissions.[1] Expectations were great, and it was evident that one of the key players would be the People's Republic of China. After all, China—the world's largest emitter of greenhouse gases[2]—has taken huge strides in the past decade, toughening up its environment protection laws, fighting pollution, planting forests, and investing aggressively in renewables and energy efficiency. In the lead-up to Copenhagen, China announced it would cut its carbon intensity by 40–45 percent below 2005 levels by 2020.[3]

In the end, Copenhagen was a flop. No binding treaty covering both developed and developing countries was established, nor was a deadline set for reaching such an agreement. No global target for 2050 was created. Major emitters reached an accord that committed the world to halting the rise in global temperatures to two degrees Celsius, but the measures it contained were insufficient to deliver that outcome.

There were many reasons for the disappointment of Copenhagen, but in the public mind at least, China bore a good deal of responsibility. Beijing's aversion

Michael Fullilove is the Director of the Global Issues Program at the Lowy Institute for International Policy in Sydney, Australia and a Nonresident Senior Fellow in Foreign Policy at the Brookings Institution in Washington, D.C. He may be reached at mfullilove@lowyinstitute.org.

Copyright © 2011 Center for Strategic and International Studies
The Washington Quarterly • 34:3 pp. 63–85
DOI: 10.1080/0163660X.2011.587980

to quantifiable commitments led it to oppose one that didn't even apply to China directly, namely the critical pledge that by 2050 rich countries would cut emissions by 80 percent compared to 1990 levels. China and other high-emitting developing states opposed the principle of international verification, agreeing only to "international consultations and analysis." The Chinese argued for removing references to Copenhagen as a way-stage on the path to a legally binding treaty. China's representatives hardly acquitted themselves well in the conference venue either, with Premier Wen Jiabao dodging important meetings with U.S. President Barack Obama and sending a more junior official instead.[4] Britain's then-Climate Change Minister, Ed Miliband, called China out on its behavior, leading China's Foreign Ministry to reply: "The remarks against China by an individual British politician contained obvious political schemes to shirk responsibilities toward the developing countries and provoke discord among the developing countries."[5] That politician is now Britain's alternative Prime Minister. A widely-cited article in The Guardian was headed: "How do I know China wrecked the Copenhagen deal? I was in the room."[6]

China's predicament in Copenhagen illustrated in miniature many of the features of China's awkward relationship with the United Nations: the high hopes; the genuine, often startling, progress; the continuing disconnect between China's weight and its strategy; the conflicting desires to be seen as a great power and a poor country; the tacking between arrogance and uncertainty; and the hurt feelings on both sides when expectations are crushed. Copenhagen put the following question in front of the international community: how far has China progressed toward achieving the status of a "responsible stakeholder," urged on it by then-U.S. Deputy Secretary of State Robert Zoellick in 2005?[7] Examining China's approach to the UN could help answer that question. The research for this article, which was supported by the Australia–China Council, included two dozen confidential interviews conducted in 2009–2010 in Beijing, New York and Washington, D.C.

Is China a Power or a Player?

Any account of recent shifts in Beijing's foreign policy behavior has to begin with its deeply impressive economic performance. In three decades, China has remade its economy, driven extraordinary productivity increases, and in so doing raised hundreds of millions of people out of poverty. Now this country of 1.3 billion people is achieving an economic weight befitting its huge size. In 2009, its gross domestic product (GDP) was the third largest in the world in dollar terms; if measured in terms of purchasing power parity, it was the second largest. Annual GDP growth in the last five years has averaged more than 11 percent. China is the third largest importer and second largest exporter in world merchandise trade. The country is laying roads and high-speed rail, building airports, and expanding shipping at a frenetic pace. In 2011, its hoard of foreign exchange reserves passed the $3 trillion mark—more than double the amount of second-placed Japan. The historian Paul Kennedy has predicted that by the time the UN celebrates its centenary in 2045, "China could well constitute the largest economic and productive force in the world, bigger even than the United States."[8]

China's economic strength is mirrored in its growing military capabilities. The United States' 2010 Quadrennial Defense Review recorded that "China is developing and fielding large numbers of advanced medium-range ballistic and cruise missiles, new attack submarines equipped with advanced weapons, increasingly capable long-range air defense systems, electronic warfare and computer network attack capabilities, advanced fighter aircraft, and counter-space systems." These developments boost China's ability to project power within East Asia and around the world.[9]

While China has arrived as a great power, that does not necessarily mean that it is destined for global or even regional hegemony, as some enthusiasts maintain. China's façade conceals some worrying divisions, including those between rich and poor as well as between the coast and interior. As German strategist Josef Joffe observes, China needs to resolve "the pernicious dynamics of authoritarian modernization—war, revolution, and upheaval—that eventually befell imperial Germany, Japan, and Russia." It also needs to manage two awkward demographic realities: the country has become powerful while many of its people remain poor, and it will get old before it gets rich. Still, even if we don't credit straight-line projections, one thing is clear: China is a global player, with vast implications for the international system.[10]

China has a strong hand; how it will play that hand in the future is not so obvious. There is a notable dualism to China's approach. On one hand, Deng Xiaoping bade his countrymen to keep their heads down and their eyes on the prize of economic development. Deng's so-called 24-character strategy was: "Observe calmly; secure our position; cope with affairs calmly; hide our capacities and bide our time; be good at maintaining a low profile; and never claim leadership." Even as this approach has given way to the newer Chinese foreign policy doctrines of "peaceful rise" and "harmonious world," the Chinese leadership remains overwhelmingly focused on domestic issues.[11] One Chinese interviewee told the author: "Beijing is not psychologically ready to be an active global player."[12]

In their recent paper *Global Governance 2025*, the U.S. National Intelligence Council and the EU Institute of Strategic Studies reported: "Many of our Chinese interlocutors see mounting global challenges and fundamental defects in the international system but emphasize the need for China to deal with its internal problems."[13] The Chinese Communist Party's first priority is regime continuity, which rests on a stable society, a viable economy, and GDP growth sufficient to keep unemployment down. One Beijing observer even asserted to this author that "all of the leadership's top ten issues are domestic."[14] For much of the time, China's external preoccupations are to prevent other powers from trespassing on what it regards as its domestic issues—such as Taiwan and Tibet—and to secure the energy and other resources necessary to power growth. Chinese foreign policy is neither expansionist nor extreme; in many ways, China has been slow to claim the influence it clearly deserves.

On the other hand, it is impossible to miss China's rising confidence and international ambition, even if they sit alongside strains of caution and insecurity. In the past decade, China has expanded its clout in Southeast Asia; thickened its ties with U.S. treaty allies such as South Korea and Australia; and extended its influence in Africa, Latin America, the Middle East, and in new Asian institutions such as the East Asia Summit and the Shanghai Cooperation Organization. One American China-watcher observed to this author that global issues such as international architecture and the world economy have moved to the center of discussions between Washington and Beijing.[15] This may now be the most important bilateral relationship in the world.

Sometimes, Chinese assertiveness spills over into bluster. Some long-time observers are pessimistic about the direction of Chinese foreign policy. Scholar David Shambaugh has noted that in 2010, frictions manifested in many of China's relationships: with Europe and India, with countries in Southeast Asia, Latin America, and Africa—even with Russia. The U.S. relationship has proven bumpy. Beijing stage-managed President Obama's 2009 visit to China in a way that minimized Obama's effect on his Chinese audience and complicated things for him with his American audience. China snubbed Defense Secretary Robert Gates and arced up over relatively routine matters such as the president's meeting with the Dalai Lama and Taiwan arms sales. Meanwhile, the relationship with Tokyo suffered a significant setback after Japan's Coast Guard detained a Chinese trawler captain in the East China Sea near the disputed Senkaku / Diaoyu Islands. China's uncompromising response, including the suspension of ministerial talks and (reportedly) halting rare earth exports, elevated a third-order issue to a matter that had to be resolved by the heads of government.[16]

The explanations for this passage of behavior are diverse, including the ongoing leadership transition, Chinese nationalism, and the country's successful navigation of the global financial crisis. A recent Stockholm International Peace

Research Institute (SIPRI) policy paper by Linda Jakobson and Dean Knox makes a powerful argument for the increasing pluralization of Chinese foreign policy, as authority over the policymaking process fractures and the leadership is required to accommodate various institutions, factions, and ideologies. Certainly, there is an uneven quality to China's present foreign policy: usually quiet but occasionally strident; usually cautious but occasionally combative; always prickly; and never entirely predictable.[17]

China and the United Nations

The same ambivalence is evident in China's relations with the international organization. China has quickened the pace of its interactions with the UN in recent decades, exerting increasing influence in UN forums on matters it cares about. Yet, it has so far refused to assume the responsibilities incumbent upon a global power, and to nurture the international system it hopes to help to lead.

The clashes between Chinese and UN forces in the Korean War and the occupation of the China seat at the UN by Taiwan aroused a great deal of hostility in the People's Republic toward the UN. Since Beijing acquired the seat in 1971, however, the acrimony has faded and it has steadily joined specialist organs and acceded to treaties. Samuel Kim charted the progression of its approaches, from "system-transforming" prior to 1971 to "system-reforming" in the 1980s to "system-maintaining" in the 1990s. From the mid-1990s, this progression has accelerated.[18]

The Chinese began to appreciate two particular advantages the UN offers them as an arena for power politics. First, the UN's structural design tends to mitigate unipolarity: in the General Assembly, the United States is one of a multitude; even in the Security Council, it is at best first among equals. Second, the UN is hierarchical—and China is on the top rung of the hierarchy. Professor Rosemary Foot notes that Beijing "values the status benefits it derives from permanent membership of the Security Council, and especially the influence that comes with the privilege of the veto."[19]

The Stakeholder Spectrum

How should we assess China's current mode of engagement with the UN? The approach differs depending on the issue. One can draw a continuum of China's UN behavior, on which the position of a policy or tool is determined by the degree of openness to, engagement with, and burden-sharing on behalf of the international organization. Let's call it China's "stakeholder spectrum."

ENGAGEMENT

Diplomats

Peacekeeping

Responsibility to protect

Security Council behaviour

Iran

North Korea

Human rights

DISENGAGEMENT

Diplomats

At the end of the spectrum denoting maximum engagement, we can place the issue of the caliber of China's UN diplomats. There is no question that the quality of people China sends to New York, both as diplomats and officials, has improved markedly. Thirty years ago, argues Shambaugh, "China's representatives rarely said a word—and when they did speak it was pure propagandistic rhetoric carefully prepared in Beijing. No press conferences were offered to foreign media, at home or abroad." Kim quoted one UN representative describing the old approach like this: "They come. They smile. They leave."[20] Five years ago, a UN insider told this author: "Beijing's representatives used to be woefully unqualified, faceless apparatchiks. Now they are very sharp. China used to take a prophylactic approach to placing people in the UN, asking 'how can we protect our people from outside influence?' Now they want to spread their influence." This year, another remarked that China's diplomats are "extraordinarily sophisticated and capable," with "a clear strategic vision." A diplomat from a Permanent Five (P5) country told this author "they will ride their instructions from Beijing" in order to strike deals they believe are in the Chinese interest.[21]

Elements of the old mentality still persist. In September 2010, China's most senior UN official, Under-Secretary-General for Economic and Social Affairs Sha Zukang, was forced to apologize after a toast he offered to Secretary-General Ban Ki-moon at an alpine retreat descended into a drunken tirade against the UN, Americans, and Ban himself.[22] Yet Sha's behavior was the exception that proved the rule. In general, China's representatives have become much more skillful at promoting their country's interests at headquarters and contributing to the organization's work.

Whether the newer generations have noticeably different views on foreign policy is another question, and one on which interviewees differed. Several think-tankers expressed the view that younger officials are less orthodox in their thinking and more likely to recognize "the legitimacy quotient" in being a global power. But P5 officials interviewed by this author thought otherwise. One volunteered that "a generational divide does not show up in meetings. Junior and mid-level Chinese diplomats are often franker than their elders but they are also well-trained and obedient."[23]

Peacekeeping

Also toward the engagement end of the spectrum is China's contribution to UN peacekeeping. This may be the field in which Beijing has moved the furthest toward engagement with the organization. Prior to admission and even into the 1970s, Beijing was apt to characterize peacekeeping operations as imperialist adventures. A government publication claimed that the establishment of the Special Committee for Peacekeeping Operations, for example, aimed to turn the UN into a "U.S.-controlled headquarters of international gendarmes to suppress and stamp out the revolutionary struggles of the world's people."[24] The ice began to crack in the 1980s, as Deng Xiaoping led China to work toward peaceful relations with the West, including through participation in international organizations. China first voted for peacekeeping operations, then began to support them financially, then joined the Special Committee, and finally deployed its first personnel to peacekeeping operations, in Africa and the Middle East.[25] In the past two decades, the Chinese contribution has grown further, notwithstanding China's traditionally rock-solid commitment to the concept of state sovereignty and the norm of non-interference in the internal affairs of other states.

> Peacekeeping may be the field in which Beijing has moved the furthest.

Beijing's support for UN peace missions has not been limited to traditional peacekeeping operations. It has included post-conflict multi-dimensional peacekeeping—such as in Darfur, Sudan, and the Democratic Republic of Congo—and transitional administrations such as in Cambodia (despite China's association with the Khmer Rouge) and East Timor. Beijing has traditionally referred to three principles, derived from UN peacekeeping history and its own foreign policy theories, when deciding whether to authorize and participate in peacekeeping operations: host-country consent; use of force only in self-defense; and the involvement of regional actors. However, these are being applied flexibly and pragmatically, rather than uniformly. For example, China has voted for resolutions authorizing the use of military force and participated in peacekeeping missions involving the use of force.[26] China has also partly overcome its allergy toward peacekeeping missions in countries that recognize Taiwan. In the 1990s, for instance, China vetoed or threatened to veto proposed missions in Haiti, Guatemala, and Macedonia on this basis; now China supports the current UN operation in Haiti despite that country's continuing diplomatic ties with Taipei.[27]

Beyond generally supporting peace missions, China has begun to staff them, and in increasing numbers. Over the past two decades, Chinese supporters have overcome internal objections based on history, ideology, and concerns from some Chinese military officers about casualties. China now deploys more military and police personnel to UN peacekeeping operations than any other permanent member of the Security Council, and it is the 15th-largest contributor overall. Furthermore, China has invested substantially in training facilities for its peacekeepers who are, according to SIPRI, "among the most professional, well-trained, effective and disciplined contingents in UN peacekeeping operations."[28] This increase—achieved in the absence of external pressure—was an adroit move. Peacekeeping is a prominent UN activity and China's preparedness to take on more of it has added to its prestige within the organization.

Nevertheless, progress made in Chinese peacekeeping should not be overstated. China's Security Council votes on peacekeeping are still conditioned by its traditional regard for state sovereignty and, to some extent, the principles of host-country consent, minimum use of force, and regional involvement. Although the number of Chinese personnel deployed in UN missions is high relative to the past and to other P5 countries, it remains small in absolute terms: 1,995 people as of September 2010. (There are well over two million personnel in the Chinese armed forces.) Finally, rather than deploying combat troops, Beijing has so far focused on enablers, military observers, and police.[29] Nevertheless, the shift is important.

Responsibility to Protect

A little further down the continuum is China's treatment of the concept of "the responsibility to protect" (R2P). R2P is the emerging norm that after Somalia, Bosnia-Herzegovina, Rwanda, and Kosovo, a collective international responsibility exists in cases of genocide, ethnic cleansing, and widespread violations of human rights. The idea is that while states retain the primary responsibility for protecting their citizens, in the event that states are unwilling or unable to protect their people, then sovereignty must yield to the international responsibility to protect them.

Given R2P's potential to violate the traditional concept of state sovereignty, China has exhibited discomfort about some of its ramifications, but it has not opposed it outright. Former foreign minister Qian Qichen sat on the UN panel that endorsed R2P, and China supported the concept at the 2005 World Summit and in Security Council Resolution (SCR) 1674 (2006). However, Beijing has taken a very limited view of its application, emphasizing the importance of building capacity within states to prevent atrocities. It is, says analyst Sarah Teitt, "wary of competing interpretations of R2P, and resists attempts to expand R2P and initiatives to 'invoke' R2P in Council proceedings." Beijing regularly stresses the need for the Council to act "prudently" in the case of emerging crises, and comments that "states must refrain from using R2P as a diplomatic tool to exert pressure on others."[30]

> China has exhibited discomfort about R2P, but it has not opposed it outright.

Many believed that, in light of the imbroglios in Afghanistan and Iraq, the high-water mark for humanitarian intervention had passed. Nevertheless, the occurrence of significant popular protests and armed resistance this year against the Qaddafi regime in Libya, and the regime's violent response, has brought the concept of R2P back to the fore in New York. In February, China joined the rest of the Security Council in adopting SCR 1970 (2011), which imposed an arms embargo on Libya as well as a travel ban and assets freeze on the Libyan leadership, while referring the situation to the International Criminal Court. The following month, China abstained from voting on SCR 1973 (2011), which imposed a no-fly zone over Libya's territory and tightened sanctions against the regime. Both resolutions invoked the responsibility to protect civilians.

China's willingness to support the first resolution and not to veto the second represents, on the face of it, a significant advance. This is, as Alex J. Bellamy has noted, the first time in history that the Council has "authorized force against a functioning government to protect civilians." On the other hand, China's behavior was the product of very particular circumstances. The support of the Arab League and African Union for a no-fly zone was plainly critical to China's willingness not to block SCR 1973. Indeed its permanent representative Li Baodong stated that China "attached great importance" to the positions of the two regional organizations. The resolutions had broad international, as well as regional, support, which made them harder to veto.[31] We can also speculate that China was reluctant to be isolated on the Libya issue in a way that would draw attention to the heavy hand it applies to its own citizens. The Arab Spring has proven to be highly infectious. To stand with Qaddafi against international sanctions might have had unpredictable consequences. Far better to present a small target internationally and get on with the business of keeping a lid on any unrest at home.

It would be wrong, then, to see China's recent performance as indicating a significant change of heart on R2P. (Indeed, Beijing has gone out of its way to criticize Western-led air strikes against Libyan government targets.)[32] China was boxed in on this occasion, but its essentially skeptical approach remains. Whether the passage of these two resolutions has created a lasting precedent, with repercussions for China as well as the rest of the world, will depend in large part on the outcome of the conflict in Libya.

Security Council Behavior

The extent and limits of China's shift toward UN engagement can be discerned in its general behavior on the Security Council, on which it is the only Asian member of the P5, as well as the only developing country. Historically, China was a passive Council member, rarely seeking to shape the agenda. China used its veto significantly less than any other permanent member, casting only four between 1971 and 2002, for example, compared to the United States' 75. It generally abstained from or did not participate in voting unless the issue touched on sovereignty questions, especially if they might influence Taiwan or Tibet. Votes that were registered were usually preceded by a *pro forma* statement that no precedent was thereby established. In the past decade and a half, however, Beijing's representatives have displayed much greater confidence in the Council chamber. China is increasingly willing to take the lead on issues and behave more like a normal great power.[33]

> China is increasingly willing to take the lead on issues and behave more like a great power.

The PRC is adamant about the "One China" policy. But at the UN, there are now two Chinas: General Assembly China, which is more rigid and doctrinaire; and Security Council China, which is more pragmatic and flexible. P5 diplomats and UN officials observe that China's Security Council diplomacy is smarter and more subtle than the Russians', and that "the Chinese are more reliable in sticking to deals they have struck."[34] China has developed a good working relationship in the Council with the United States, although it is far from the vaunted "P2" (the P2 being the UN version of the much-discussed "G2"). Day-to-day diplomacy in the Security Council is still coordinated between China and Russia on one hand and among the United States, the United Kingdom, and France on the other. China has partly overcome its instinctive opposition to resolutions passed under Chapter VII of the UN Charter, which empowers the Council to take measures to maintain international peace and security. For example, China voted for resolutions to support the Australian-led INTERFET force in East Timor in 1999 and to establish the UN Transitional Administration in East Timor later that year.[35] On September 12, 2001, it joined with the rest of the Council to condemn the 9/11 attacks as a threat to international peace and security and recognize the right of self-defense against such attacks (SCR 1368 (2001)).

On the other hand, China remains disengaged from many issues of importance where they do not trespass directly on its core interests. Notwithstanding its support for SCR 1368, for instance, it is not active on Afghanistan, being mainly concerned to keep Pakistan happy with the Council's deliberations. To the relief of Sri Lanka, China refused to allow the Security Council to discuss the bloody denouement of that government's operations against the Tamil Tigers in 2009.[36] The majority of the action on the most difficult issues comes from the United States, the United Kingdom, and France. China is as uncomfortable as ever at being isolated (except on sovereignty issues), which limits its negotiating power. In other words, it is occupied largely with protecting its interests and those of its allies rather than projecting its influence—much less doing too much to strengthen the international system. In the words of a P5 diplomat, "China is mostly in defensive mode, intent on preventing things that hurt it, rather than achieving things that help it."[37]

China has a mixed record on the treatment of so-called "pariah" states in the Council, as analysts Stephanie Kleine-Ahlbrandt and Andrew Small have previously chronicled.[38] After the Tiananmen Square massacre of 1989 and the Soviet Union's fall two years later, Beijing strengthened its relationships with dictatorships. The connections with energy-rich outcasts such as Sudan and Burma further deepened in the 1990s, as China's growth surged and its appetite for resources grew. "By late 2004 and early 2005," argue Kleine-Ahlbrandt and Small, "China's support for pariah regimes had taken a defensive—even ideological—turn."[39] In 2005, Beijing praised Uzbekistan's violent handling of anti-government protests and welcomed President Robert Mugabe of Zimbabwe for a state visit in the middle of his government's campaign to demolish the homes of opposition supporters. In the Security Council, it consistently resisted, diluted, or abstained from supporting resolutions that threatened real consequences for the government of Sudan over the horrors occurring in the Darfur region.

Since then, however, concerned about the fragility of some of the regimes it supports and conscious of its international reputation, China has begun to condition its support in some cases. During its 2007 Security Council Presidency, for example, it prodded Khartoum into accepting a joint UN–African Union mission to support the implementation of the 2006 Darfur Peace Agreement. No doubt China was keen to polish its international reputation in the lead-up to the Beijing Olympics, as well as to prevent the spread of instability in a region in which it had substantial investments.[40] Yet its record remains patchy, as demonstrated by the October 2010 draft report of an expert panel which revealed that Chinese bullets had been used in attacks on UN peacekeepers in Darfur. (Chinese diplomats in New York reportedly threatened to veto the renewal of the panel's mandate unless the language of the report was modified.)[41]

In the Security Council, China has edged up the spectrum in the direction of engagement with the international community. Yet it has not gone far enough. China's larger interests should dictate a more pronounced move. Beijing's economic and political interests with pariah states are significant, but they are dwarfed by its ties with Western countries and the reputational cost of cozying up to the Mugabes and Than Shwes of the world. P5 diplomats see little evidence that their Chinese colleagues share this view, especially in relation to the country's reputation. One told this author that "there is a certain amount of fatigue at always being the defender of unpleasant regimes—but it should not be overstated and it is rarely decisive."[42]

A senior UN official characterized shifts in China's Security Council behavior as important, but "incremental, not tectonic."[43] China has become a more skillful and effective player, but it has not developed a policy that is consonant with its expanded interests. This tension is evident in its approach to the two critical issues of the Iranian and North Korean nuclear programs.

Iran

There is no definitive proof that Iran is engaged in a program to develop nuclear weapons. However, there is widespread international concern that Tehran's effort to gain mastery of the nuclear fuel cycle through its civilian nuclear program will put it within easy technical reach of a nuclear weapon at some point in the future. Because Iran has been caught lying about the full extent of its nuclear effort, there are also real concerns about the existence of parallel, covert programs to produce such weapons.[44]

China's performance on this issue has been unimpressive; one senior UN official, otherwise complimentary about Beijing, says "the Chinese think they can play fast and loose on Iran."[45] Under sustained pressure from Western powers, China supported three rounds of Security Council resolutions in 2006–2008 imposing sanctions on Iran for violating its obligations to the International Atomic Energy Agency (IAEA) and the UN, but only after working with Russia to dilute the sanctions and drain them of effect. The two countries pursue what the Crisis Group has called "a delay-and-weaken" strategy.[46]

The latest iteration of this took place in 2009–2010, after the revelation of Iran's underground uranium enrichment facility near Qom. In June 2010, after months of haggling, China and Russia signed on to the most comprehensive Security Council sanctions package yet, targeting Iran's financial system in particular. Analyst Michael Swaine argues that China surprised many observers by agreeing to the latest resolution, but it did so only after receiving various incentives and assurances, and to avoid isolation in light of Russia's anticipated shift to support the sanctions.[47] The financial sanctions appear to be having a greater effect on the regime in Tehran than anticipated. That has not stopped the wrangling, however. In October 2010, the Obama administration concluded that Chinese firms were assisting Iran to develop its missile technology and nuclear weapons, and asked Beijing to get the companies to desist.[48]

Beijing's interests on the Iranian nuclear issue are not, of course, identical to Western ones. China is a significant consumer of Iranian energy, receiving 11 percent of its crude oil from Iran (its third-largest supplier after Saudi Arabia and Angola) and taking a keen interest in the country's oil and gas reserves. It sees Iran as an important partner in the Middle East and something of a counterweight to U.S. dominance in the region, as well as a potential partner in Central and Southwest Asia. With its strong historical attachment to the principle of state sovereignty, China is more prone to rest on Iran's right under the Nuclear Non-Proliferation Treaty to develop nuclear technology for peaceful purposes. Given China's own experiences as the target of sanctions—especially the Western sanctions imposed after Tiananmen Square and the revelations of missile sales to Pakistan—it is most reluctant to agree to sanctions and far more inclined to the diplomatic track.[49] (Almost every Chinese interviewee reminded this author of the history of sanctions directed against China.)

> Human rights is the issue on which China is most disengaged.

However, this approach seems short-sighted given what is at stake for the world, and for China, as a key player in the international system. An Iranian bomb would embolden a regime with links to Hezbollah and other terrorist groups, endanger strategic waterways, threaten regional states (including, importantly, other key suppliers of energy to China in the Persian Gulf), and contribute to regional and global nuclear proliferation. The idea of a powerful state balancing the United States in the Middle East may seem superficially attractive to Beijing, but as one Chinese strategist commented to this author, "a nuclear-armed stronghold of anti-Americanism in the region would presage a bleak future for China, not least because of rising oil prices."[50] Swaine notes it would also degrade "China's status as one of only a handful of nuclear powers, undermine the NPT, and (perhaps most importantly) add to the number of nuclear armed powers in close proximity to China... This would reduce China's relative influence as a major power, worsen its immediate threat environment, and arguably destabilize the larger global security environment."[51]

In the long term, China's approach is risky; in the short term, it is undermining its relationships with the West and its international reputation. Surely, if it is opposed to the development of Iranian nuclear weapons and also keen to minimize the use of force to this end by the United States or Israel, then it should maximize its diplomatic solidarity with Western powers in the Security Council. China has legitimate national interests to protect, but it could take a larger view of those interests.

North Korea

The North Korean nuclear weapons program is, in the words of a UN official, "much more dangerous for the Chinese" than the Iranian program.[52] During the Cold War, China was North Korea's chief protector and quartermaster, in an alliance that was said to be as "close as lips and teeth."[53] Much of the ideological camaraderie has evaporated since Deng's reforms, but history and personal ties remain—as a Chinese interviewee told this author, "many Chinese lost their lives in the Korean War, and most Chinese people would be reluctant to give up their old friends."[54]

The last five years have defined more clearly the limits of Beijing's conversion.

Political and security interests are, naturally, dominant. China is loath to see a collapsed state on the Korean peninsula—with resulting refugee flows and security implications—or reunification with South Korea that would mean China had to suffer American GIs on its eastern border. On the other hand, how comforting is it to suffer a highly unpredictable, not to say unhinged, family-owned regime on your eastern border? There is also the question of the thickness of China's economic ties with the two Koreas: there are 25 times as many commercial flights between China and South Korea as between China and North Korea, and 50 times as much total trade.[55]

Chinese frustration with North Korea emerged at the time of Pyongyang's 2006 nuclear test, which President Hu Jintao was reportedly notified about only 20 minutes in advance. Publicly, Beijing criticized the move as "brazen"; in the Council, it supported sanctions against the hermit kingdom.[56] In 2009, Pyongyang mounted another series of provocations, launching a rocket, walking out of the Six-Party Talks, and testing a second nuclear device. Again Beijing was critical of its ally, yet this time it was determined not to damage its bilateral relationship (or, perhaps, expose its own lack of influence over Pyongyang) with the kind of overt rhetoric it had employed three years earlier. The Crisis Group reports that there is an unusually public debate in Beijing over ties with North Korea between "traditionalists," who propose the continued provision of support to North Korea, and "strategists," who propose a harder line.[57] Strategists even go so far as to say (as one did to this author): "North Korea is the bad guy and South Korea is the good guy. China has to be on the right side of history."[58]

This debate became more prominent in 2010, against the backdrop of an awkward political transition in Pyongyang and North Korea's sinking of the South Korean corvette *Cheonan* in March, with 46 fatalities. China's response—that North Korea's role was unproven—lacked credibility and was characterized by President Obama as "willful blindness."[59] U.S. and South Korean naval maneuvers off the Korean peninsula followed, but Chinese diplomatic maneuvers in New York confined the Security Council's

> China continues to define its national interests narrowly.

response to a weak statement from its president. Thus, the international organization's response to the unprovoked sinking of a warship with substantial loss of life—a clear threat to international peace and security, one would have thought—was a presidential statement that did not name the attacker and was labeled by *The New York Times* as "absurdly, dangerously lame."[60] Similarly, China refused to allow the Council to condemn North Korea's further provocations in late 2010, when it revealed the existence of a new uranium enrichment facility and launched a deadly artillery barrage at South Korea.[61]

Human rights

The issue at the very end of China's stakeholder spectrum, on which it is the most disengaged, is human rights. Beijing is largely hostile to independent international scrutiny of its own deeply flawed human rights record, as seen in its reaction to the awarding of the Nobel Peace Prize to dissident Liu Xiaobo. China is a member of the UN's Human Rights Council (HRC), and it allows itself to be subjected to the Universal Periodic Review (UPR) mechanism, by which the HRC assesses the human rights records of all member–states every four years. China's participation in the UPR is to be welcomed, and it is right that the resulting reports praise the country's remarkable achievements in poverty reduction. However, human rights groups note that China takes a high-handed and defensive approach to the process.[62]

> China wants respect, but not responsibility.

Beijing is equally obstructionist when it comes to the scrutiny of other countries' human rights records, especially its friends and allies. In 2007, for instance, China was the strongest advocate of proposals to curtail the ability of the HRC to monitor human rights in individual countries, only relenting in exchange for the withdrawal of its special rapporteurs on Belarus and Cuba. In the Security Council, China usually works with Russia to prevent the consideration of human rights violations in places such as Zimbabwe and Darfur. Burma is a good example: in 2007, Beijing and Moscow vetoed a draft Security Council resolution critical of the military junta; in the last few months of 2010, China mounted "a high-octane, Western-style diplomatic effort" to oppose U.S. moves to pressure the country's leaders by launching a commission of inquiry into possible war crimes they may have committed.[63]

Through the approach it has taken in the HRC, the old Commission on Human Rights, the Security Council, and the General Assembly, China has played a critical role in wearing down Western capitals on human rights issues and pushing human rights further to the periphery of UN debate.

Two Steps Forward, One Step Back

In Western countries, there is sometimes a tendency to lay the blame for any friction in the China relationship on our own politicians. No doubt this is sometimes justified. But China, too, has a choice as to how it comports itself. Its behavior helps determine how other states react to it. Its approach to the international organization helps determine its influence over the organization—and in the world.

In the past quarter-century, China has become a far more active and effective player in the UN, sometimes even outperforming the United States. It has changed the way it does business (through its diplomats and on the Security Council) and the business it does (for example, in the areas of peacekeeping and the responsibility to protect). Yet, the last five years have defined more clearly the limits of Beijing's conversion. Some of the items on China's UN agenda (for example North Korea), that were previously moving up the stakeholder spectrum have now stabilized and even slipped down a little. China continues to define its national interests narrowly and pursue them with an uncompromising resolve. China wants respect, but not responsibility. It is reluctant to bind its own freedom of movement and subsume it within international institutions in the way the United States did after the Second World War, even though Washington's relative power was far greater then than Beijing's is now.

Some analysts will say that a rising China will want to reshape the UN in coming years. It may well. However, one should not underestimate either the extent to which the structures and practices of the organization already accord with China's interests, or the difficulty of altering those structures and practices to favor China further over the certain objections of the rest of the P5, other important powers such as Japan and India, and other member states.

There are debates in China over these issues, and in some ways they mirror Western debates: there are "idealists" who study and promote the UN, and "realists" who scold them for neglecting Chinese power or compromising Chinese values.[64] But the Chinese debate is heavily tilted toward UN skeptics and away from UN groupies—"there are not many John Ikenberrys in China," observed one academic to this author.[65] Many foreign policy actors in Beijing regard the West's "responsibility" agenda as an attempt to retard China's rise. In the aftermath of the Copenhagen debacle, for example, the debate in China was less about whether Wen Jiabao's concessions went far enough and more about whether they went too far.

None of this is to say that China's interests coincide exactly with Western interests. They do not, and we should not expect China to act exactly as the West does. Nor should we ask China to advance global interests at the expense of its national interests. But as China's wealth and power grow, so will its interests expand. A middle-power foreign policy is inadequate for a great power.

> Beijing may put forward its own, quite different, stakeholder spectrum.

If China is to help run the international system, then it has a stake in strengthening it. Beijing needs to strike a new balance between its traditional economic as well as security concerns and the broader imperatives it must now satisfy, including stable great-power relations, non-proliferation, and developing its international prestige. China's UN performance has largely escaped scrutiny in the last two decades, with the world's head turned first by U.S. power and then by U.S. overreach. That pattern will not hold. The old principle—that with power comes responsibility—requires China to move up the stakeholder spectrum.

On the other hand, the West needs to be careful what it wishes for. Western countries want Beijing to be more responsible and active, but they don't like it when Beijing is more assertive. China's version of "stepping up" is not necessarily the same as the West's. Professor Pang Zhongying has argued that a stronger China may be less anxious about external powers intervening in China's domestic affairs, but also less fussy about observing the principle of non-interference in *other* states' domestic affairs.[66] How would the West feel about

China involving itself in the Middle East peace process, for example, or participating in "coalitions of the willing" that intervened in other countries?

In other words, the responsibilities—and prerogatives—of a stakeholder are open to interpretation. In the future, Beijing may put forward its own, quite different, stakeholder spectrum.

Notes

1. Greg Picker and Fergus Green, "Comprehending Copenhagen: a guide to the international climate change negotiations," Lowy Institute for International Policy, 2009, p. 4: http://www.lowyinstitute.org/Publication.asp?pid=1177.

2. "Comparison of Carbon Dioxide Emissions, 1965–2009: United States and China," http://www.instituteforenergyresearch.org/wp-content/uploads/2010/06/carbon-dioxide-emissions-1965-2009-US-China.jpg; "Carbon dioxide emissions (CO2), thousand metric tons of CO2 (CDIAC)," Millennium Development Goals Indicators, http://mdgs.un.org/unsd/mdg/SeriesDetail.aspx?srid=749&crid=.

3. James Fallows, "China's Silver Lining," *The Atlantic*, June 2008, http://www.theatlantic.com/magazine/archive/2008/06/china-8217-s-silver-lining/6808/; Deborah Seligsohn, Rob Bradley, and Jonathan Adams, "Fact Sheet: Energy and Climate Policy Action in China (Update)," World Resources Institute, November 5, 2009, http://www.wri.org/stories/2009/11/fact-sheet-energy-and-climate-policy-action-china-update; Thomas Friedman, "The New Sputnik," *The New York Times*, September 26, 2009, http://www.nytimes.com/2009/09/27/opinion/27friedman.html; Michael Fullilove and Fergus Green, "Talks should at least be a big step on the way," *The Sydney Morning Herald*, December 8, 2009, p 11.

4. "Climate change after Copenhagen: China's thing about numbers," *The Economist*, December 30, 2009, http://www.economist.com/node/15179774?story_id=15179774; "Copenhagen Accord faces first test," International Institute for Strategic Studies, *Strategic Comments* 16, January 2010, http://www.iiss.org/EasySiteWeb/GatewayLink.aspx?alId=40511; Fareed Zakaria, "Clash of the Titans: How the Democratic Republic of Google is testing China's appetite for democracy itself," *Newsweek*, January 15, 2010, http://www.newsweek.com/2010/01/14/clash-of-the-titans.html; Jonathan Watts, "Speculation over change in role for Chinese climate negotiator," *The Guardian*, January 5, 2010, http://www.guardian.co.uk/environment/2010/jan/05/he-yafei-china-climate-negotiator.

5. Ed Miliband, "The road from Copenhagen," *The Guardian*, December 20, 2009, http://www.guardian.co.uk/commentisfree/2009/dec/20/copenhagen-climate-change-accord; for Foreign Ministry Spokesperson Jiang Yu's response to the British accusation that China "hijacked" negotiations at the Copenhagen Climate Change Conference, see http://www.fmprc.gov.cn/eng/xwfw/s2510/t647058.htm.

6. Mark Lynas, "How do I know China wrecked the Copenhagen deal? I was in the room," *The Guardian*, December 22, 2009, http://www.guardian.co.uk/environment/2009/dec/22/copenhagen-climate-change-mark-lynas.

7. Robert B. Zoellick, "Whither China: From Membership to Responsibility?" (speech, National Committee on U.S.-China Relations, New York, September 21, 2005), http://www.kas.de/wf/doc/kas_7358-544-1-30.pdf.

8. Xiaochao Li, "Further expanding momentum of China's economic recovery in the first quarter of 2010," National Bureau of Statistics of China, April 15, 2010; "Gross

domestic product 2009," World Bank, December 15, 2010, http://siteresources. worldbank.org/DATASTATISTICS/Resources/GDP.pdf; "Gross domestic product 2009, PPP," World Bank, December 15, 2010, http://siteresources.worldbank.org/ DATASTATISTICS/Resources/GDP_PPP.pdf; "GDP growth (annual %)," World Bank, http://data.worldbank.org/indicator/NY.GDP.MKTP.KD.ZG; "World trade developments in 2008," World Trade Organization, http://www.wto.org/english/res_e/ statis_e/its2009_e/its09_world_trade_dev_e.htm; Fareed Zakaria, "The Recession's Real Winner: China turns crisis into opportunity," *Newsweek,* October 17, 2009, http:// www.newsweek.com/2009/10/17/the-recession-s-real-winner.html; Kevin Yao and Langi Chiang, "China FX reserves soar past $3 trillion, add to inflation," *Reuters,* April 14, 2011, http://www.reuters.com/article/2011/04/14/us-china-economy-reserves-idUSTRE 73D1T620110414; Hugh White, "Power Shift: Australia's Future between Washington and Beijing," *Quarterly Essay* 39, September 2010, pp. 11–13; Paul Kennedy, *The Parliament of Man: the United Nations and the Quest for Global Government* (London, Allen Lane, 2006), p. 245.

9. U.S. Department of Defense, *Quadrennial Defense Review Report,* February 2010, p. 31, http://www.defense.gov/qdr/images/QDR_as_of_12Feb10_1000.pdf; U.S. Department of Defense, *Military Power of the People's Republic of China 2008,* p. i, http://www.au.af.mil/ au/awc/awcgate/dod/china_report_2008.pdf; M. Taylor Fravel, "China's Search for Military Power," *The Washington Quarterly* 31, no. 3 (Summer 2008), http://twq.com/ 08summer/docs/08summer_fravel.pdf.

10. Josef Joffe, "The Default Power: The False Prophecy of America's Decline," *Foreign Affairs* 88, no. 5 (September/October 2009): p. 5; Steven Mufson and John Pomfret, "There's a new Red Scare. But is China really so scary?" *Washington Post,* February 28, 2010, http://www.washingtonpost.com/wp-dyn/content/article/2010/02/26/ AR2010022602601.html.

11. Deng Xiaoping quote from Stephanie Kleine-Ahlbrandt and Andrew Small, "China's New Dictatorship Diplomacy: Is Beijing Parting with Pariahs?" *Foreign Affairs* 87, no. 1 (January/February 2008): p. 41.

12. Confidential interview, Beijing, June 3, 2010.

13. National Intelligence Council (NIC) and the European Union Institute for Security Studies (EUISS), *Global Governance 2025: At a Critical Juncture,* September 2010, p iii, http://www.dni.gov/nic/PDF_2025/2025_Global_Governance.pdf.

14. Confidential interview, Beijing, June 4, 2010.

15. Confidential interview, Washington, D.C., October 7, 2009.

16. David Shambaugh, "The Chinese tiger shows its claws," *Financial Times,* February 17, 2010, http://www.ft.com/cms/s/0/d55d5578-1b62-11df-838f-00144feab49a.html; Michael Fullilove, "Frustrated US struggles to open dialogue with China," *The Sydney Morning Herald,* February 22, 2010; Josh Rogin, "Gates snub raises tough questions about China ties," *Foreign Policy,* June 4, 2010, http://thecable.foreignpolicy.com/posts/2010/06/03/ gates_snub_raises_tough_questions_about_china_ties; Sachiko Sakamaki and Takashi Hirokawa, "Kan, Wen move to resolve China-Japan dispute," *Bloomberg,* October 6, 2010, http://www.bloomberg.com/news/2010-10-05/kan-wen-meeting-positive-for-japan-china-s-bilaterial-ties-sengoku-says.html.

17. Linda Jakobson and Dean Knox, "New Foreign Policy Actors in China," Stockholm International Peace Research Institute, Policy Paper 26, September 2010, pp. vi-vii, http://books.sipri.org/files/PP/SIPRIPP26.pdf; Fareed Zakaria, "The Beijing Blues," *Newsweek,* June 4, 2010, http://www.newsweek.com/2010/06/04/the-beijing-blues.html; Zakaria, "Clash of the Titans"; Fareed Zakaria, "Growing Pains," *Newsweek,* February 5, 2010, http://www.newsweek.com/2010/02/04/growing-pains.html; Kerry Brown, "The

Power Struggle among China's Elite," *Foreign Policy*, October 14, 2010, http://www.foreignpolicy.com/articles/2010/10/14/the_power_struggle_among_chinas_elite.

18. Samuel S. Kim, "China and the United Nations," in *China Joins the World: Progress and Prospects*, eds. Elizabeth Economy and Michel Oksenberg (New York: Council on Foreign Relations Press, 1999); Bates Gill and Chin-hao Huang, "China's expanding role in peacekeeping: prospects and policy implications," Stockholm International Peace Research Institute, Policy Paper no. 25, November 2009, p. 4, http://books.sipri.org/files/PP/SIPRIPP25.pdf; "China's growing role in UN peacekeeping," International Crisis Group, Asia Report no. 166, April 17, 2009, pp. 3–5, http://www.crisisgroup.org/ ~/media/Files/asia/north-east-asia/166_chinas_growing_role_in_un_peacekeeping.ashx.

19. Rosemary Foot, "Chinese strategies in a US-hegemonic global order: accommodating and hedging," *International Affairs* 82, no. 1 (January 2006): p. 82.

20. David Shambaugh, "Reforming China's diplomacy," Asia Research Centre, January 31, 2010, http://openarchive.cbs.dk/bitstream/handle/10398/8013/Hele_discussion_paper.pdf?sequence=1; Kim's report of representative's quote reproduced in Michel Oksenberg and Elizabeth Economy, *Shaping US-China relations: a long-term strategy* (New York: Council on Foreign Relations, 1997), p. 29.

21. Confidential interviews, New York, October 1, 2009 and September 30, 2009.

22. Colum Lynch, "Exclusive: China's John Bolton," *Foreign Policy*, September 9, 2010, http://turtlebay.foreignpolicy.com/posts/2010/09/08/chinas_john_bolton; "UN diplomat Sha Zukang sorry for rant," *The Australian*, September 15, 2010, http://www.theaustralian.com.au/news/world/un-diplomat-sha-zukang-sorry-for-rant/story-e6frg6so-1225922928310.

23. Confidential interviews, New York, September 30, 2009 and October 1, 2010.

24. Tiewa Liu, "Marching for a more open, confident and responsible great power: explaining China's involvement in UN peacekeeping operations," *Journal of International Peacekeeping* 13, no. 1–2 (January 2009): pp. 121–122. See also International Crisis Group, "China's growing role in UN peacekeeping," pp. 3–5.

25. International Crisis Group, "China's growing role in UN peacekeeping," pp. 5–10; Gill and Huang, "China's expanding role in peacekeeping," pp. 4–5.

26. International Crisis Group, "China's growing role in UN peacekeeping," pp. 2–3, 19–25.

27. Gill and Huang, "China's expanding role in peacekeeping," pp. 13–14; United Nations, "UN Mission's Summary detailed by Country," September 30, 2010, http://www.un.org/en/peacekeeping/contributors/2010/sept10_3.pdf. China had a sizeable contingent of riot police in Haiti but it withdrew them in the weeks following the January 2010 earthquake: see Colum Lynch, "In surprise move, China withdraws riot police from Haiti," *Foreign Policy*, March 25, 2010, http://turtlebay.foreignpolicy.com/posts/2010/03/25/in_surprise_move_china_withdraws_riot_police_from_haiti.

28. United Nations, "Ranking of military and police contributions to UN operations," September 30, 2010, http://www.un.org/en/peacekeeping/contributors/2010/sept10_2.pdf; Gill and Huang, "China's expanding role in peacekeeping," pp. 5–7 and 26–27.

29. Gill and Huang, "China's expanding role in peacekeeping," p. 11; Weidi Xu, "Yaobai yu Panghuang zhong de Tansuo: Lianheguo Weihe Xingdong Mianlin de Kunnan yu Tiaozhan. [Exploration in vacillation and hesitation: the difficulties and challenges facing U.N. peacekeeping operations]," *World Economics and Politics*, no. 5, p. 9; United Nations, "Ranking of military and police contributions to UN operations"; International Institute for Strategic Studies, *The Military Balance* 110 (Routledge,

2010), p. 465; International Crisis Group, "China's growing role in UN peacekeeping," pp. 27–30.

30. Sarah Teitt, "China and the Responsibility to Protect," Asia-Pacific Centre for the Responsibility to Protect, December 19, 2008, pp. 2, 9, 10, http://www.responsibility toprotect.org/files/China_and_R2P%5B1%5D.pdf; "Implementing the Responsibility to Protect: Asia-Pacific in the 2009 General Assembly Dialogue," Asia-Pacific Centre for the Responsibility to Protect, October 2009, p. 18, http://www.responsibilitytoprotect.org/ index.php/component/content/article/172-asia-pacific/2667-implementing-the-responsibility-to-protect-asia-pacific-in-the-2009-ga-dialogue-.

31. Alex J. Bellamy, "The Responsibility to Protect: Libya and Beyond," *e-International Relations*, March 30, 2011, http://www.e-ir.info/?p=7912; "Security Council approves 'no-fly zone' over Libya," SC/10200, March 17, 2011, http://www.un.org/News/Press/ docs/2011/sc10200.doc.htm; Douglas H. Paal, "China: Mugged by Reality in Libya, Again," Carnegie Endowment for International Peace, April 11, 2011, http:// www.carnegieendowment.org/publications/index.cfm?fa=view&id=43554.

32. "Foreign Ministry Spokesperson Jiang Yu's Remarks on Multinational Military Strike against Libya," Ministry of Foreign Affairs of the People's Republic of China, March 21, 2011, http://www.fmprc.gov.cn/eng/xwfw/s2510/t808094.htm; "Chinese President says force is no solution to Libyan issue," March 30, 2011, Chinese Embassy in the United States, http://www.china-embassy.org/eng/zgyw/t811054.htm.

33. Samuel S. Kim, "China in world politics," in *Does China Matter? A Reassessment*, eds. Barry Buzan and Rosemary Foot (London: Routledge, 2004), pp. 43–46. In his analysis of voting records of the permanent five, Kim excludes a 1981 volley of U.S. and Chinese vetoes during deliberations on nominations for Secretary-General on the grounds that these "behind-the-scenes" votes are not included in official UNSC documentation.

34. Confidential interview, New York, October 1, 2009.

35. Bates Gill, "China Becoming a Responsible Stakeholder," Carnegie Endowment for International Peace, June 11, 2007, p. 5, http://carnegieendowment.org/files/Bates_ paper.pdf.

36. Jenny Page, "Chinese billions in Sri Lanka fund battle against Tamil Tigers," *The Times*, May 2, 2009; Security Council Report, "Sri Lanka," Update Report no. 1, June 4, 2009, http://www.securitycouncilreport.org/atf/cf/%7B65BFCF9B-6D27-4E9C-8CD3-CF6E4F F96FF9%7D/Update%20Report%204%20June_Sri%20Lanka.pdf.

37. Confidential interview, New York, October 1, 2009.

38. Kleine-Ahlbrandt and Small, "China's New Dictatorship Diplomacy."

39. Ibid, p. 42.

40. Ibid, pp. 46–47. See also Gill and Huang, "China's expanding role in peacekeeping," p. 14; International Crisis Group, "China's growing role in UN peacekeeping," pp. 20–21.

41. Peter Ford, "China dismisses UN report that Chinese bullets were used in Darfur," *Christian Science Monitor*, October 21, 2010, http://www.csmonitor.com/World/2010/ 1021/China-dismisses-UN-report-that-Chinese-bullets-were-used-in-Darfur.

42. Confidential interview, New York, September 30, 2009.

43. Confidential interview, New York, October 2, 2009.

44. Anthony Bubalo and Michael Fullilove, "Iran, the international community and the nuclear issue: where to next?" Lowy Institute for International Policy, December 2005, p. 3, http://www.lowyinstitute.org/Publication.asp?pid=330.

45. Confidential interview, New York, October 1, 2009.

46. Willem van Kemenade, "China vs. the Western Campaign for Iran Sanctions," *The Washington Quarterly* 33, no. 3 (July 2010): p. 108, http://twq.com/10july/docs/10jul_va nKemenade.pdf; Michael D. Swaine, "Beijing's tightrope walk on Iran," Carnegie Endowment for International Peace, *China Leadership Monitor*, no. 33, June 28, 2010, pp. 7–8, http://carnegieendowment.org/files/CLM33MS.pdf; "The Iran nuclear issue: the view from Beijing," International Crisis Group, Asia Briefing no. 100, February 17, 2010, p. 13, http://www.crisisgroup.org/en/regions/asia/north-east-asia/china/B100-the-iran-nuclear-issue-the-view-from-beijing.aspx; "Factbox: EU, U.N. and U.S. sanctions against Iran," *Reuters*, September 23, 2010, http://www.reuters.com/article/2010/09/23/us-thyssen-iran-sanctions-idUSTRE68M26320100923.

47. Swaine, "Beijing's tightrope walk on Iran," p. 8.

48. John Pomfret, "U.S. says Chinese businesses and banks are bypassing U.N. sanctions against Iran," *The Washington Post*, October 18, 2010, http://www.washingtonpost.com/wp-dyn/content/article/2010/10/17/AR2010101703364.html.

49. International Crisis Group, "The Iran nuclear issue: the view from Beijing," pp. 5, 11 n. 103; Swaine, "Beijing's tightrope walk on Iran," pp. 1–2; van Kemenade, "China vs. the Western Campaign for Iran Sanctions," p. 103.

50. Confidential interview, Beijing, June 3, 2010.

51. Swaine, "Beijing's tightrope walk on Iran," p. 3.

52. Confidential interview, New York, October 1, 2009.

53. Marc Lanteigne, *Chinese foreign policy: an introduction* (London: Routledge, 2009), p. 114.

54. Confidential interview, Beijing, June 2, 2010.

55. Korea Airports Corporation aviation statistics, http://www.airport.co.kr/doc/www_eng/info/E040105.jsp; Korea Konsult, International timetables to/from North Korea, http://www.koreakonsult.com/hur-tar-man-sig-dit_eng.html; International Monetary Fund, *Direction of Trade Statistics Yearbook: 2010*.

56. Kleine-Ahlbrandt and Small, "China's New Dictatorship Diplomacy," pp. 44–45.

57. "Shades of red: China's debate over North Korea," International Crisis Group, Asia Report no. 179, November 2, 2009, p. i, http://www.crisisgroup.org/en/regions/asia/north-east-asia/china/179-shades-of-red-chinas-debate-over-north-korea.aspx.

58. Confidential interview, Beijing, June 3, 2010.

59. Andrew Jacobs and David E. Sanger, "China returns U.S. criticism over sinking of Korean ship," *The New York Times*, June 29, 2010, http://www.nytimes.com/2010/06/30/world/asia/30korea.html.

60. "Security Council Blinks," *The New York Times*, July 10, 2010, http://www.nytimes.com/2010/07/11/opinion/11sun3.html.

61. Peter S. Green and Frances Yoon, "China declines to condemn North Korean shelling as South prepares drill," *Bloomberg*, December 19, 2010, http://www.bloomberg.com/news/2010-12-19/china-declines-to-condemn-north-korean-shelling-as-south-prepares-drill.html.

62. Thomas Lum and Hannah Fischer, "Human rights in China: trends and policy implications," *CRS Report for Congress*, renowned RL34729, January 25, 2010, http://www.fas.org/sgp/crs/row/RL34729.pdf; Human Rights Watch, "UN: Nations show true colors at rights review," February 13, 2009, http://www.hrw.org/en/news/2009/02/13/un-nations-show-true-colors-rights-review.

63. Richard Gowan and Franziska Brantner, "A global force for human rights? An audit of European power at the UN," European Council on Foreign Relations, 2008, p. 37, http://www.ecfr.eu/page/-/documents/30b67f149cd7aaa888_3xm6bq7ff.pdf; Sarah E. Mendelson, "Dusk or Dawn for the Human Rights Movement?" *The Washington*

Quarterly 32, no. 2 (April 2009): p. 109, http://twq.com/09april/docs/09apr_Mendelson.pdf; "Security Council fails to adopt draft resolution on Myanmar, owing to negative votes by China, Russian Federation," SC/8939, January 12, 2007, http://www.un.org/News/Press/docs/2007/sc8939.doc.htm; Warren Hoge, "U.S. rebuke to Myanmar is defeated by U.N. vetoes," *The New York Times*, January 13, 2007, http://www.nytimes.com/2007/01/13/world/asia/13nations.html; Colum Lynch, "U.S. push for Burmese war crimes probe hits Chinese wall," *Foreign Policy*, October 24, 2010, http://turtlebay.foreignpolicy.com/posts/2010/10/24/us_push_for_burmese_war_crimes_probe_hits_chinese_wall.

64. For an excellent analysis of the various schools of Chinese foreign policy thought, see David Shambaugh, "Coping with a Conflicted China," *The Washington Quarterly* 34, no. 1 (Winter 2011): pp. 7–27, http://twq.com/11winter/docs/11winter_Shambaugh.pdf.

65. Confidential interview, Beijing, June 3, 2010.

66. Pang Zhongying, "China's Non-Intervention Question," *Global Responsibility to Protect* 1, no. 2 (March 2009): pp. 237–252, especially pp. 249–252.

William Varettoni

Crimea's Overlooked Instability

It was, perhaps unfortunately, a picture broadcast round the world. Ditching decorum, Ukraine's protesting parliamentarians hurled eggs, set off smoke-belching flares, poured glue in voting machines, and duked it out (literally) within their legislative chamber on April 27, 2010. At issue was the parliament's ratification of a lease extension for Russia's Black Sea Fleet in the Ukrainian port of Sevastopol, Crimea. The lease was due to expire in 2017, but will now (most likely, although nothing is ever set in stone in Ukrainian politics) continue through 2042. In exchange, Ukraine will receive a roughly 30 percent discount on natural gas imports from Russia, worth up to $40 billion over 10 years.[1] If it works as advertised, Kyiv sold some of its sovereignty for a stronger economy. Given the current economic environment, few dispassionate observers would begrudge Ukraine this singular tradeoff.

The basing extension is unlikely to be reversed, and Crimea has once again receded from the headlines. This is both disappointing and dangerous, because the fate of the Black Sea Fleet is far from the most combustible issue facing Crimea. Crimea is at much greater risk for violence than most people assume, including those in Moscow feting the lease extension, because of two flawed tenets of conventional wisdom.

The first holds that Russia wants to annex Crimea and is merely waiting for the right opportunity, most likely under the pretense of defending Russian brethren abroad. This would be accurate if it could be done with no consequences. But Russia has seen that overt action in Crimea is a strategic loser, as evidenced by its

William Varettoni is a former Foreign Affairs Analyst at the U.S. Department of State and currently a PhD candidate at the Maryland School of Public Policy. The views expressed are the author's alone and do not reflect those of the U.S. government, and the interviews referenced herein reflect only those conducted as a private citizen. He may be reached at wvarettoni2@gmail.com.

Copyright © 2011 Center for Strategic and International Studies
The Washington Quarterly • 34:3 pp. 87–99
DOI: 10.1080/0163660X.2011.588128

> **R**ussia alone is not the gravest threat; it has seen that overt confrontation in Crimea is a strategic loser.

failed attempt to assert claim to the sandbar island of Tuzla. This breach of Ukrainian sovereignty received nearly universal condemnation by Ukrainians, who supported the deployment of troops to secure the island. Russia is a bigger beneficiary of the status quo than Kyiv, and has greater incentives to avoid significant changes. The Sevastopol base extension only reinforces this. Furthermore, overt Russian action also risks undermining one of its major foreign policy successes—its effective use of soft power in Crimea. Russia's deployment of soft and covert power has given it significant control in Crimea at a fraction of the physical and political cost of the so-called frozen conflicts in Transnistria and Georgia. This may prove a tempting template for expanding its influence within its neighbors.

The second tenet, common both inside and outside of Ukraine, is that Russia poses the greatest security threat to Crimea. While Russia's behavior in Crimea undeniably encourages instability, it is only part of the problem. Crimea is far more complex, and at risk of civil conflict, than most recognize. Ethnic tensions, a widening fissure between Islamic and Orthodox Christian populations, disinformation campaigns, and cycles of elite-manipulated instability all threaten to throw Crimea into a downward spiral of civil violence. These issues have festered since Ukraine's independence and are likely to get worse under President Viktor Yanukovych. They are ignored at great peril. The much-hyped fear of overt Russian intervention in Crimea is far more likely to result from these unaddressed issues spiraling out of control than from any deliberate plans coming out of Moscow.

Where on Earth is Crimea ... and Why Does It Matter?

Roughly the size of the state of Delaware, the Autonomous Republic of Crimea is a peninsula in southern Ukraine extending into the Black Sea. It has significant local governing autonomy according to a local constitution, but is ultimately subject to the Ukrainian constitution and law. Home to approximately 2.5 million people, it is the only area within Ukraine that has an ethnic Russian majority (approximately 60 percent). This percentage is higher in the independently-administered city of Sevastopol, leased home of the Russian Black Sea Fleet. Ten to 12 percent of the population is Crimean Tatar, an indigenous ethnic group brutally deported to Central Asia under Stalin during World War II. They were allowed to return beginning in the late 1980s, bringing their Islamic identity with them. The remainder of the population is mostly ethnic Ukrainians; by and large, they identify culturally with the Slavic Russians on the peninsula.

Russian is the predominate language. Russian media dominates, and its attendant propaganda is pervasive. Crimea had been part of the Russian empire since 1783, but was transferred by Nikita Khrushchev to the Ukrainian Soviet Socialist Republic in 1954. The rationale for the transfer is debated, but it clearly made sense from a practical standpoint given the direct land connection and utilities access of Crimea to the Ukrainian SSR (Crimea is not physically connected to Russia). At any rate, since it was internal to the Soviet Union, few attached any particular significance to the move at the time. The 1954 transfer—particularly with regard to Sevastopol—has been contested by some in the Russian parliament and several prominent Russian politicians.[2] However, post-Soviet treaties between Ukraine and Russia clearly state that Russia acknowledges Ukraine's control of Crimea.

Today, as in Soviet times, Crimea is known as a prime tourist destination; as such, coastal land is highly sought for private vacation homes, hotels, and resorts. Repatriating Crimean Tatars seek land for restitution and resettlement. For the last decade and a half, they have grown ever more frustrated with the corrupt land trade in Crimea which has largely excluded them. There is no fully functioning land register, so it is not possible to know with certainty who owns which piece of property. Business and land deals are opaque. Many Tatars have taken to squatting illegally on land plots to claim them, sometimes with success. This naturally pits Tatars against Slavs, a situation exacerbated by the fact that—at least culturally—Crimean Tatars are Muslim and Slavs are Orthodox Christian. These tensions regularly lead to minor clashes, but ultimately elites on both sides pull their constituencies back from the brink.

Crimea's small size belies its importance as a flashpoint for Russia–Ukraine and Russia–NATO relations, for the presence of the Russian Black Sea Fleet, for its role as a laboratory for the trial and use of Russian soft power, and because of its sharp ethnic and religious divide between a previously deported indigenous population and the descendants of the Slavs who moved into their vacant homes. It is precisely the interaction of these factors that destabilizes Crimea.

Russia Delights in the Status Quo

As noted, conventional wisdom holds that Moscow is merely waiting for the right opportunity to annex Crimea. If the move were consequence-free, that would certainly be the case. But any attempt to take over Crimea would carry severe penalties, and Russia knows it. On balance, Russia has greater incentives to maintain the status quo than even Kyiv. Among the benefits of the status quo for Russia: unfettered use of its naval base, formidable sympathies from the local population based on years of soft power, a relatively free economic hand, and a political pressure point against Kyiv and NATO. The disincentives to annexation are more compelling still: a history of failed Crimean separatist movements, demonstrated backlash from mainland Ukrainians to overt Russian action in Crimea, and an (almost) inevitable Western response.

Far From Fleeting

Russia's marquee interest in Crimea is the Black Sea Fleet's base in Sevastopol. By treaty, Russia leases its Black Sea Fleet facilities from Ukraine. Moscow has a relatively free hand in operating the fleet, so even if Sevastopol became Russian territory, not much would change from a practical standpoint.

The presence of the Black Sea Fleet in Crimea is first and foremost a political mission, with the fleet often dismissed by many observers as largely militarily insignificant. While certainly not the most potent of Russia's naval forces, the fleet nonetheless helped handily sink the Georgian Navy in 2008. Russia has publically signaled its intention to augment the fleet's capability. To this end, Russia is negotiating a deal with France to acquire four amphibious assault ships, an intention announced ominously a mere year after the 2008 Russo-Georgian War.[3] Further still, the communications and energy pipelines which crisscross the Black and Mediterranean seas will continue to proliferate. A Russian naval presence could sabotage these vital seabed connections. All this is to say that Russian naval power in the region is, and will continue to be, strategically important.

As a military installation, Sevastopol is one of the best naval ports in the region. Its deep harbors and porous rock formations have made it a naval gem for hundreds of years. Neither Russia's Black Sea port of Novorossiysk nor Abkhazia's Ochamchire come close to Sevastopol as a military installation.[4] Nonetheless, expansions in both ports would correct the over-concentration of forces in Sevastopol. Russia's move to diversify its basing makes military sense, and in no way signals that Sevastopol is militarily "optional."

The fleet is also important for cultural reasons. Much significance is attached to Crimea in Russian and Soviet military history and nostalgia. Crimean residents hold a tremendous amount of pride about the military glories of yesteryear, albeit many of them glorious defeats. Crimea was an important symbol of the Russian empire, representing its furthest reach to the southwest. While the decay of the fleet is plain to see, this seems to have done little to color perceptions of the past. These feelings might peacefully exist within the Ukrainian state, but the 2008 war in Georgia brought the dangers of this relationship into sharp relief.

Since Georgian forces were attacked with Black Sea Fleet ships, Georgia would have been within its rights to attack Sevastopol. There is no getting around the fact that the return address for Russia's Black Sea Fleet is Ukrainian territory, and this could have disastrous consequences for Ukraine's relationships with its littoral neighbors. Russia's staging attacks from Ukrainian territory could subject Ukraine to attack or pull Ukraine into a conflict. During the war in Georgia, then-Ukrainian president Viktor Yushchenko threatened (by presidential decree) to deny the return to port of ships involved in the hostilities. This was patently unenforceable and derisively dismissed by Moscow; Yushchenko abandoned the effort. The incident served to highlight how entrenched the fleet is in Sevastopol and how little power Kyiv has over the prerogatives of the Russian navy.

Russia's Soft Power Success

When one thinks of Russia exerting control within its "sphere of interest," it's generally fairly obvious. Think of the frequent Ukrainian gas crises or the frozen conflicts in Transnistria, Nagorno–Karabakh, South Ossetia, and Abkhazia. In diplomacy, Russia tends to come across as assertive and bullying, at least according to many of its neighbors. Probably the last thing one thinks of in the Russian toolbox is soft power. But that's exactly what it has been using—to great effect—for years in Crimea. The local population, by and large, is strongly attracted to Russia for its politics, culture, economics, and shared history.

Russia's soft power focuses most intensely on three areas: media, culture, and history. The Russian press and television dominate Crimea, despite attempts by the Ukrainian government to ratchet down exposure. Almost the entire population of Crimea regularly speaks Russian, so it is instinctive to gravitate to Russian film and television. The Black Sea Fleet, businessmen, and NGOs with Russian affinities sponsor a number of local publications and television stations. In addition to attracting Crimeans to a Russian point of view, the media relentlessly advances two dangerous themes: 1) Kyiv is to blame for Crimea's

Internal tensions are actually more likely to be the source of near-term conflict.

socio-economic problems (given the paralysis in Kyiv since the 2005 Orange Revolution, this is not a hard sell); and 2) radical Islam is spreading among Crimean Tatars. Both of these themes reinforce the attractiveness of Russia, which is seen as an oasis of relative stability and security for Slavs.

Russia established a branch of Moscow State University in Sevastopol, and sponsors a number of cultural organizations.[5] At a minimum, it influences several groups of so-called "Russian Cossacks." These have been variously described to me as boy scouts, paramilitaries, thugs-for-hire, and everything in between. Depending on which of the two dozen or so organizations you are talking about, you can find ones that exhibit these qualities. Their unifying theme is that they celebrate Russian culture and vow to protect it. Alarmingly, when there are violent clashes between Tatars and Slavs, a Russian Cossack group is almost always present. If Moscow ever had the intention to destabilize Crimea with a measure of plausible deniability, these would be its shock troops.

Historically, Sevastopol was one of 12 "Hero" cities in the former Soviet Union, so honored for heroic defensive efforts during World War II. Political speeches and public events, to an inordinate degree, still focus on this history. Even more than distracting from the problems of the present, this constant look backward creates a sense of unity and pride among Slavs in Crimea. At the same time, it reinforces the "us versus them" divide between Tatars and Slavs; despite many Tatars fighting valiantly on the Soviet side, Stalin accused Crimean Tatars of collaborating with the Nazis. He deported their entire community to central Asia in 1944. Some estimate that 40–50 percent of the Tatar population died during the process of deportation and exile.[6]

Russia's willingness to use soft power to entice sympathies appears to be a significant departure from its generally assertive (and sometimes belligerent) foreign policy. This is not to say that soft power was by design or its first choice, but rather the next thing to try when it became clear that hard power would not work. As Russia takes stock of its foreign policy wins and losses, I believe that the successful tactics used in Crimea may prove an attractive template to be deployed elsewhere. The use of soft power has allowed Russia to both achieve and sustain a status quo that benefits it as much, and likely more, than overt territorial aggregation. And it's done so at a fraction of the economic and political cost of frozen conflicts.

Both a Hong Kong and a Trump Card

Russia and Cyprus (that is to say, Russia and Russia) are consistently top investors in Crimea, with 37 and 11 percent of foreign investment, respectively.[7] And that does not include all of the shadow investments floating in. Land, as Crimea's most attractive asset, enjoys an opacity in ownership and transfer that makes it a currency onto itself. Crimea's former Minister of Tourism estimated that more than three quarters of tourism-related revenues were off the books. In this shadow economy, Russian businessmen are not considered foreign investors, and enjoy the same corrupt access to local authorities as Ukrainian businessmen. As Paul Goble, who served as special adviser on Soviet nationality issues and Baltic affairs to Secretary of State James Baker, phrased it, Crimea functions a bit like a Hong Kong for Russian businesses.[8] It is a trading point for illegal trafficking, and its territory is used to evade taxes and avoid much official scrutiny from both Ukrainian and Russian authorities.

While tracking illicit business is exceedingly difficult, it stands to reason that Crimea is seen as a far more legitimate place to do business than the so-called "frozen conflict" territories. Yet, local governance is weak and corruption is rampant. In this atmosphere, it is difficult for the Ukrainian state to exert control over the Crimean economy, and Russia enjoys levels of market access not too far removed from where it would be if it owned the territory outright.

In dealing with Kyiv, and to some extent NATO, Russia has this Crimean trump card. Moscow can, and does, drum up street protests in short order. The Russian apparatus has shown remarkable responsiveness to Ukraine's prospects for joining NATO; when Ukraine flirts seriously, Crimea comes alive with anti-NATO protests. More frighteningly than street protests, Russia could handily send Crimea into violent chaos if it chose to. It might not be able to control it once it started, but it can certainly foment it. Better still from Russia's standpoint, it can do so while still maintaining plausible deniability (say, through the use of Russian Cossack cultural groups). Russia can play, or threaten to play, this trump card if Kyiv ever gets too far out of line. The effects of instability in Crimea could quite realistically influence Ukrainian elections, cause the collapse of a governing coalition, or scuttle NATO accession negotiations.

Hard Power Fell on Hard Times

Beyond the myriad incentives Russia has in preserving the status quo, it also faces pronounced disincentives to overt action in Crimea. The most devastating is the prospect of permanent bad blood between Ukraine and Russia. Russia got a glimpse of this during the 2003 Tuzla Island dispute. Without Ukrainian consent, Russia began building a causeway to the island, which is basically a sandbar in the Kirch strait separating Crimea from mainland Russia. Ukraine took a strong stand that its territorial integrity had been violated and sent troops to protect the island.[9] More importantly, Ukrainian public opinion—even in the Russian-sympathetic eastern part of Ukraine—was overwhelmingly in support of Ukraine sending troops and asserting its integrity. The clear lesson for Moscow was that overt actions which encroach on Ukraine's sovereignty risk alienating its important support base in mainland Ukraine.

Another strong disincentive is the likely response of the international community. As evidenced during the war in Georgia, overt Russian action in Crimea would likely wreak havoc on Russian financial markets and foreign investment in the country. Russia might also risk provoking economic sanctions if it is seen as an aggressor toward Ukraine, although European reliance on Russian gas would limit this leverage. Whereas Western diplomatic resolve was lacking in the case of the war in Georgia, Ukraine is both closer and of far greater importance to the West. Russia must certainly fear a united diplomatic front from the West, something it has not fully seen since the Cold War.

> **B**y rhetoric alone, politicians and the press have created a phantom radical Islamic crisis.

The prospect of separatism might be attractive to Moscow, except that Russia has already watched it fail in Crimea. The best hope of a viable separatist movement rose and fell on the tenure of Yuriy Meshkov as president of Crimea. In response to his separatist agenda, Kyiv and its domestic intelligence apparatus stepped in and abolished the presidential institution, and Meshkov's two year tenure, in 1995. This devolved significant authority back to Kyiv. It is not clear to what degree Meshkov was supported by Moscow, but the failure of the separatist regime certainly limited Russia's options for influence going forward.

The last significant disincentive is perhaps Russia's own history, and Vladimir Putin has shown a predilection for historical lessons. From the fall of the Soviet Union through the 2008 war in South Ossetia, Russia's involvement in the so-called frozen conflicts in Transnistria and Georgia showed the world that Russia has an assertive foreign policy and is a force to be reckoned with. But the cost of this support, both in terms of diplomatic and economic capital, has taken a toll on Russia. There are few tangible benefits in the frozen territories beyond using them as smuggling corridors. The costs of confrontation are high, and the Kremlin must be searching for a better way to strengthen its "sphere of influence." It's difficult to imagine a Russian appetite for yet another frozen conflict, this time on the territory of Crimea.

Given the tangible benefits of maintaining the status quo, and these substantial disincentives to overt action, it is unlikely Russia will—by design—move to change the current situation in Crimea.

Europe's Next Religious Fault Line?

> The prospects that all Crimean Tatars will refrain from violence dim with each passing day.

While the potential use of military force has dominated discussion about Crimea, internal tensions are actually more likely to be the source of near-term conflict. As Crimean Tatars repatriated from Central Asia beginning in the late 1980s and early 1990s, they sought land to settle on and compensate them for the assets taken when they were deported. The Ukrainian state agrees in principle that this should happen, but in practice the process has been halting and slow. While the Crimean Tatar population's grievances are socio-economic, the Slavic population is focused on the Tatars' Muslim identity, in opposition to their Christian one.[10]

The most striking—and disturbing—aspect of public discourse in Crimea is the notion that radical Islam is spreading among Crimean Tatars. Invariably, Russian-leaning (or simply pro-Slav) politicians during interviews spend a substantial part of the time talking about it, and papers and television are rife with hype about the threat. In fact, there is little evidence that there is an outsized incidence of radicalization, even less than one would expect in a typical pluralist society. There are, of course, a handful of strict Wahhabis.[11] There are even some groups, such as Hizb ut-Tahrir, with radical rhetoric. But there is no indication of violent tendencies, and there has not been any violence carried out specifically in the name of Islam. By rhetoric alone, politicians and the press have created a phantom crisis to drive a wedge between Slavs and Tatars.

The Tatars have seen little progress in terms of land, employment, and opportunity over the last decade and a half; as a result, their frustration has grown.[12] The 2010 election of Viktor Yanukovych has only increased their anger and despair, as few see any hope of their situation improving under the Russia-friendly president.[13] They take as early evidence Yanukovych's appointment of Anatoliy Mogilev as interior minister.[14] Mogilev was responsible for a violent crackdown on Crimean Tatars in 2007 and has been accused by Tatars and others of human rights abuses while heading internal security in Crimea.[15]

Tatar passions have been kept in check largely by the persuasiveness of their leader, Mustafa Jemilev. A veteran of the Crimean Tatar movement, he wields a tremendous amount of moral authority. But he's 67 years old and (from what I've seen) a heavy smoker. Nearly every faction of Crimean Tatars I interviewed talked about succession and how their sub-group had a shot at gaining the leadership role.

While the Crimean Tatars have been remarkably cohesive as an ethnic group thus far, it is not at all clear what a post-Jemilev world will look like. Hitherto nonviolent, the prospects that all Crimean Tatars will refrain from violence dim with each passing day. While not a useful comparison, some delusional Tatars may look to Abkhazia for inspiration on how a small minority can drive out a major ethnic group and "reclaim" a territory they consider their homeland.

When Managed Instability Becomes Unmanageable

The ability to keep Crimea corrupt, and ripe for elite rent distribution, is dependent on its remaining marginally unstable. Kyiv fears violence and pronounced instability in Crimea, and tolerates local elites so long as they keep the pot from boiling over. The result is small-amplitude cycles of managed instability, driven principally by the Tatar–Slav ethnic and religious cleavage. As long as Crimea remains unstable, improving governance and political accountability will always take a distant second to physical safety in citizens' minds. And as long as they are distracted by safety concerns, the elites and their business benefactors in Ukraine and Russia can operate with a relatively free hand. The effectiveness of Russia's soft and covert power is aided tremendously by this instability, so Moscow is a key supporter of the mechanisms of managed instability.

Managed instability is coarsely and crudely maintained, with periodic clashes between Crimean Tatars and Russian Cossacks a routine part of the process. Before these incidents of minor violence get out of hand, however, elites pull their constituencies back from the brink or riot police use tear gas and force to separate the factions.[16] Tensions remain high because they are constantly reinforced by rhetoric and media reports which hype suspicions between ethnic groups.

This is possible because there are few objective facts in Crimea, and generally no reliable sources of information. This absence of reliable facts spans from land ownership to employment and state support. Because there are so many lies floating around in the free press and from the mouths of politicians, it is nearly impossible for anyone to say anything with certainty. And that is precisely why people can argue so vociferously—there are almost no accepted facts upon which to ground the debate. Each side quotes their ethnic press sources. The absence of reliable and verifiable information is a key ingredient to maintaining the "us versus them" mentality that divides the Crimean population.

Propaganda, absence of facts, and periodic clashes are central to maintaining managed instability. However, there is no immediate way to undo the damage these crude measures are visiting upon the fabric of Crimean society. If, one day, the elites are unable to pull their constituencies back from the brink, there will be no way to change mentalities forged by two decades of propaganda. How can newspapers and politicians turn around and say that they've been exaggerating Tatar radicalism or inventing statistics? These manipulations are unidirectional, and neither Kyiv nor Moscow has the ability to reverse their effects in response to escalating violence.

Despite its small size, civil violence in Crimea has profound implications for Europe, Russia specifically, and the West generally. Although in practice Crimean Tatars are largely secular Muslims, civil violence in Crimea would inevitably result in Muslim Tatars fighting Christian Slavs. A peninsula of ethno–religious conflict jutting into the heart of the Black Sea would certainly have spillover and cascading effects, and violence would likely fuel radicalization. If terrorism or organized asymmetric warfare follows, this would lead to a bloody and protracted conflict.

One frightening, but nonetheless plausible, scenario stemming from civil conflict in Crimea is that any violence on the peninsula would give Russia pretense to station additional troops in Sevastopol to protect its base and personnel. The high percentage of ethnic Russians in Sevastopol would also seek Russian protection. If violence escalated and Kyiv could not control it, Russia might fan out into other parts of Crimea in order to protect ethnic Russians from "ethnic cleansing" at the hands of Muslim Tatars. Turkey, home to a large Crimean Tatar population and sympathetic to their plight in Crimea, would certainly bristle at Russian violence visited upon Muslim Tatars, further internationalizing the conflict. If Russia acted in Crimea without Ukrainian consent, relations between the countries would be deeply damaged, and Europe might suffer yet another natural gas shutoff if Russian gas ceased to transit Ukraine. At best, this scenario ends in an uneasy stalemate and protracted negotiations. Even then, a return to violence would be far more likely given a recent history of conflict.

Whither Crimea? Crimea Withers

The internal, ethno–religious crisis facing Crimea is far greater than the debate over the future basing of the Black Sea Fleet. Now more than any time in the last half decade, Crimea is at risk for unintended civil conflict. A number of factors undergird this risk—a lack of any sustained attention to underlying internal tensions, an aging Crimean Tatar leader with unclear succession prospects, and

> Now more than any time in the last half decade, Crimea is at risk for unintended civil conflict.

a new president and interior minister seen to usher in the dimmest prospects for improvement in Tatar conditions since the collapse of the Soviet Union. Couple these underlying conditions with the managed ethno–religious instability maintained by Crimean elites (and supported by Russia), and the situation risks becoming unmanageable because of the crude ways in which the population is manipulated.

In order to stabilize Crimea, we must look beyond the conventional wisdom. Russia has significant rationale to maintain the status quo and avoid attempts to annex Crimea; it also is a major driver of instability in Crimea. But the conventional wisdom assumes Russia is the greatest security risk as well. Focusing on the Russian bugbear obscures the real danger of ethnic violence. The much-hyped fear of overt Russian action in Crimea may very well come about, but it won't be by Russian design. Instead it will be because ethnic violence spirals out of control, and Russia no longer has the option of maintaining the status quo.

Notes

1. Anatoly Medetsky, "Deal Struck on Gas, Black Sea Fleet," *The Moscow Times*, April 22, 2010, http://www.themoscowtimes.com/business/article/deal-struck-on-gas-black-sea-fleet/404501.html.
2. Vladimir Socor, "Moscow Questions Territorial Status Quo in the Crimea," *Eurasia Daily Monitor* 5, no. 92, May 14, 2008, http://www.jamestown.org/single/?no_cache=1&tx_ttnews[tt_news]=33632.
3. "Russia Orders French Mistral Amphibious Assault Ships," Defense Industry Daily, March 21, 2011, http://www.defenseindustrydaily.com/Russia-to-Order-French-Mistral-LHDs-05749/#French-Russian-Armament-Contracting.
4. Peter Cassata, "Russian Naval Base to be Built in Abkhazia," The Atlantic Council, January 27, 2009, http://www.acus.org/russian-naval-base-be-built-abkhazia.
5. Government of Sevastopol, http://sev.gov.ua/en/cityinfo/sovrem/p_3_c207/.
6. Orest Subtelny, *Ukraine: A History* (Toronto: University of Toronto Press, 2009), p. 483.
7. Government of Crimea, "Investment activity in Autonomous Republic of Crimea," http://invest-crimea.gov.ua/news_body.php?news_id=300&locale=en.
8. Paul Goble, *Window on Eurasia* blog, http://windowoneurasia.blogspot.com/.
9. Taras Kurio, *Ukraine-Crimea-Russia: Triangle of Conflict* (Stuttgart: Ibidem, 2007), pp. 79-81.
10. Alexander Bogomolov, remarks at "Islam, Orthodoxy, and the State in Crimea," Woodrow Wilson International Center for Scholars, Washington, D.C., October 9, 2007, and personal communication throughout 2007.
11. "Crimean Tatars: Three Challenges," Unrepresented Nations and Peoples Organization, January 12, 2005, http://www.unpo.org/article/1727.
12. Idil P. Izmirli, "Return to the Golden Cradle: Post-Return Dynamics and Resettlement Angst among the Crimean Tatars," in *Migration, Homeland, and Belonging in Eurasia*, eds. Cynthia J. Buckley and Blair Ruble (Washington, D.C.: Woodrow Wilson Center Press, 2008), pp. 227–264.
13. Svitlana Tuchynska, "Life 'changed for the worse' under Yanukovych, says Crimean Tatar leader," *Kyiv Post*, http://www.kyivpost.com/news/politics/detail/98553/.
14. Paul Goble, "New Ukrainian MVD Chief's Anti-Tatar Rhetoric Raises Questions about Yanukovich's Plans for Crimea," *Window on Eurasia* blog, April 11, 2010, http://

georgiandaily.com/index.php?option=com_content&task=view&id=18139&Itemid=133.

15. "Crimean Tatars Seek Criminal Case Against Ukrainian Interior Minister," Radio Free Europe / Radio Liberty, March 16, 2010, http://www.rferl.org/content/Crimean_Tatars_Seek_Criminal_Case_Against_Ukrainian_Interior_Minister/1985581.html.

16. Oleg Varfolomeyev, "Yanukovych Distances Himself From Crimea's Radical Slavs," *Eurasia Daily Monitor* 3, no. 159, August 16, 2006, http://www.jamestown.org/single/?no_cache=1&tx_ttnews[tt_news]=31977.

The Road Ahead

What's next for the Middle East as the Arab Spring turns to summer?

Juan C. Zarate and David A. Gordon

The Battle for Reform with Al-Qaeda

In the summer of 2005, Ayman al-Zawahiri, then-Osama bin Laden's Egyptian deputy, began a direct debate with the United States about the nature of reform in the Middle East. With an assault rifle in the background, al-Qaeda's number two argued that reform must be based on Shari'a and was impossible so long as "our countries are occupied by the Crusader forces" and "our governments are controlled by the American embassies." The only alternative was "fighting for the sake of God." Zawahiri concluded that "demonstrations and speaking out in the streets" would not be sufficient.[1]

That salvo in the rhetorical battle for reform set the stage for a fundamental ideological confrontation unleashed by the Arab Spring. If the wave of popular protests sweeping through the Arab world results in genuine and lasting democratic reform, the youth on the streets of Tunis, Cairo, and Benghazi will have proven Zawahiri wrong. A growing number of analysts have noted that these non-violent, secular revolutions focused on local grievances and individual rights will fatally undermine al-Qaeda's ideology and bring about its inevitable collapse.[2] Indeed, the pristine spirit of the Arab Spring is a direct challenge to al-Qaeda's central narrative. If, however, the Arab Spring leads to division, discontent, and conflict, Zawahiri's arguments will resonate and the rising tide of disillusionment could reenergize al-Qaeda's concept of reform-by-jihad in the Arab heartland.[3]

Juan C. Zarate is a Senior Adviser at the Center for Strategic and International Studies (CSIS) and the former Deputy National Security Advisor for Combating Terrorism (2005–2009). He can be reached at jzarate@csis.org. David A. Gordon is the Program Manager and a Research Assistant with the CSIS Transnational Threats Project. He can be reached at dgordon@csis.org. Both are working on a year-long CSIS study on the future of al-Qaeda and its associated movements. They would like to thank Muhammad Kirdar from CSIS for his research assistance.

The Washington Quarterly • 34:3 pp. 103–122
DOI: 10.1080/0163660X.2011.588305

The pristine spirit of the Arab Spring is a direct challenge to al-Qaeda's central narrative.

Paradoxically, the Arab Spring represents a strategic pivot for al-Qaeda and its associated movements (AQAM)—at once the moment is an existential threat to its ideology and a potential window to restore lost relevance amidst its core Sunni constituency. Given these stakes, AQAM's leaders will do everything possible to ensure the survival of their ideology, shape the narrative, and feed off the likely disillusionment arising from this chaotic period. The statements of prominent AQAM chiefs like Zawahiri and Anwar al-Awlaki—the Yemeni–American cleric and propagandist for al-Qaeda in the Arabian Peninsula—and of surrogate groups like al-Qaeda in the Islamic Maghreb (AQIM) reflect this realization and their attempts to shape the narrative of the Arab Spring.

The stakes have become even greater for AQAM after the killing of Osama bin Laden at the hands of U.S. forces in May 2011. The death of al-Qaeda's founder as well as symbolic and strategic head could spur leadership divisions and fractures in the global movement at a time when AQAM is struggling for relevance in the Arab world.[4]

For the United States, this is a strategic moment as well—where its national security interests, fundamental values, and counterterrorism goals are joined. Unlike AQAM, the U.S. government can shape the environment that follows the Arab Spring, helping to accelerate and amplify reform in support of the organic movements calling for transparent governance, individual rights, and democracy. In so doing, the United States would not only assist the new democrats of the Middle East, but also deliver a potentially fatal blow to AQAM's ideological appeal in the Arab world. The battle for reform in the Arab world has thus become a potential watershed in the long war against AQAM. The strategic moment is amplified with the loss of al-Qaeda's founder. The United States must recognize this strategic opening, and do all that it can to seize it.

On May 19, 2011, President Obama delivered remarks at the U.S. State Department intended to lay out a broad vision for U.S. policy toward the region in the wake of the popular protests. The President articulated core principles in favor of democracy and liberal values to guide U.S. policy and announced economic programs to help Egyptians and Tunisians in their quests for reform. Unfortunately the speech was overwhelmed by President Obama's injection of Israeli–Palestinian issues and the vagaries of how these policies and principles will be applied across the region.

Even with this speech, there are several reasons why exercising such strategic initiative will be difficult for Washington. With the conflict in Libya festering and dramatic events unfolding across several other countries at the speed of Twitter, U.S. policymakers risk being overwhelmed and missing the broader implications and opportunities of the current environment. A country-by-country response shaped by events of the day may be necessary, but it could impede broader strategic thinking. In addition, policymakers may elect to stand back and "do no harm" given concerns that U.S. efforts to promote reform will not be seen as credible, could taint those supported, or will be clumsily executed and thereby seen as efforts to co-opt the revolutions. Finally, the near-term imperatives of tracking down other AQAM leaders and ensuring that AQAM cannot take advantage of emerging conflict and chaos, security vacuums, and distracted regimes are necessarily the priority for the U.S. counterterrorism community. This leaves little surplus bandwidth for the complex and arduous task of devising a regional strategy that takes advantage of this moment to marginalize the movement's ideology.

This article considers the long-term implications of the Arab Spring through the lens of the war on AQAM and its ideology. This is not to suggest that the movement is a central protagonist in the unfolding manifestations of the Arab Spring, nor is this an argument for U.S. policy to be driven solely through the counterterrorism lens. This is particularly the case after the death of bin Laden, which

> **I**f the Arab Spring leads to disillusionment, it could reenergize al-Qaeda.

has made AQAM appear less relevant in the American consciousness. Instead, this article rightly asks fundamental questions about how the Arab Spring will impact AQAM in the long term, and what this moment in history means to the ideological struggle with AQAM. How has the movement's leadership already responded to the protests, and what does this indicate about their strategic reaction to the Arab Spring? What impact will the Arab Spring have on U.S. efforts to combat AQAM, and how should U.S. policies evolve? The goal is to help readers understand this strategic inflection point in the ideological battle against AQAM and to recommend steps to take full advantage of this strategic window of opportunity.

AQAM on the Eve of Revolution

To understand the future of AQAM in the wake of the Arab Spring, it is important to establish where the movement stood on the eve of the revolutions.

AQAM operatives were under enormous pressure over the past few years, particularly in the Middle East and North Africa (MENA). Security services had broken up cells and networks, and most quarters were asking fundamental questions about the legitimacy, morality, and effectiveness of the movement's tactics and strategy.

Al-Qaeda core, the group formerly led by Osama bin Laden, was ensconced in Pakistan's tribal badlands and had limited operational reach into MENA. Al-Qaeda core's rhetoric reflected this shift. In 2009, for example, only 12 percent of the propaganda messages produced by as-Sahab, al-Qaeda core's official media arm, dealt exclusively with issues in the Arab world.[5] By contrast, more than 45 percent of as-Sahab's releases that year focused on Afghanistan or Pakistan.[6]

Al-Qaeda core's Arab affiliates were only slightly better positioned to drive the jihad in MENA. Al-Qaeda in Iraq (AQI) failed to recover from its rejection by Iraqi Sunni communities during the al-Anbar Awakening and the U.S. troop surge in 2007, which left the group with a very narrow constituency.[7] Despite this setback, the group has managed to persist and sought to "demonstrate its continued relevance" through propaganda and high-profile attacks.[8]

Al-Qaeda in the Islamic Maghreb (AQIM), al-Qaeda's second official franchise, executed a devastating series of attacks immediately after its formal merger with the core in 2006. More recently, however, the group failed to maintain operational momentum in North Africa or to extend its reach into the West. Its support base in Algeria had dwindled and "AQIM failed to conduct the high-casualty attacks in Algeria that it had in previous years."[9] Unable to build support and execute attacks in its traditional area of operations, the group extended operations south into the Sahel, distancing itself from Arab North Africa.

Al-Qaeda's third official franchise, al-Qaeda in the Arabian Peninsula (AQAP), has become the most relevant AQAM network in MENA. After an unsuccessful jihad in Saudi Arabia, the battered remnants of al-Qaeda's Saudi branch merged in 2009 with Yemeni al-Qaeda members to create an increasingly capable organization under the banner of AQAP. Taking advantage of a weak central government in Sanaa, the consolidated organization carved out a foothold by "exploiting the grievances of ordinary Yeminis."[10] Although AQAP does not enjoy a broad base of support in Yemen, it has been able to exert undeniable and growing influence among certain communities. Dangerously for the United States, AQAP used Yemen as a platform to hit the homeland directly—first with the failed 2009 underwear bomber plot and later with the failed package plot in 2010. The group's rhetoric and media operations, which affected Western audiences and drew recruits to AQAM's cause, were also problematic for Washington.

Other MENA-based groups in the AQAM orbit such as the Libyan Islamic Fighting Group (LIFG) and the Egyptian Islamic Jihad (EIJ) remained largely defunct. Confronted by local security forces and faced with eroding legitimacy, many of these organizations renounced violent jihad and distanced themselves from AQAM. Members of these groups who remained committed to violence had, in many cases, matriculated to more active groups.

As a movement, AQAM was metastasizing in the run-up to the Arab Spring. This expansion was occurring on the geographic periphery of the Muslim-majority world in places like Pakistan and North America. Within MENA, however, the movement faced growing irrelevance and rejection—a process initiated by its violent overreach in Algeria, Iraq, Jordan, and elsewhere. The scores of Muslim civilians killed at the hands of al-Qaeda operatives in the region served to diminish AQAM's popularity. For bin Laden and Zawahiri, who started al-Qaeda in the hopes of bringing about regime changes in Saudi Arabia and Egypt, respectively, this lack of appeal in MENA represented a potential strategic failure. As Zawahiri noted in his manifesto, *Knights Under the Prophet's Banner*, "we must not blame the nation for not responding or not living up to the task [of waging jihad]. Instead, we must blame ourselves for failing to deliver the message, show compassion, and sacrifice."[11]

> The Arab Spring represents a strategic pivot for al-Qaeda.

What the Arab Spring Means for AQAM

The Arab Spring has redrawn the geopolitical ground of MENA. Although most analyses have rightfully focused on the implications for the countries affected and the United States, AQAM also is affected by the turmoil. And the verdict is decidedly mixed. On one hand, the Arab Spring represents a contradiction of the fundamental ideological innovations that made al-Qaeda core and the broader movement it inspired distinct from other Islamist groups. On the other hand, the revolutions may fail to give voice to the peaceful aspirations of the protesters over the long term, giving AQAM a potential opportunity to resurrect its flagging relevance in the Arab heartland.

The first ideological innovation threatened by the Arab Spring is al-Qaeda core's focus on the United States and its Western allies, commonly referred to as the "far enemy." Prior to al-Qaeda core, violent Islamist discourse focused on the "near enemy": the rulers of Muslim-majority regimes who were accused of apostasy. Despite tactical victories—such as the assassination of Egyptian President Anwar Sadat in 1981—violent Islamists were unable to achieve their strategic goal of toppling apostates and implementing Shari'a. This failure prompted bin Laden and his followers to direct their enmity toward the United States and the West, which they saw as the hidden hand propping up the apostate regimes throughout the Muslim-majority world. As bin Laden put it in his 1996 fatwa, "the situation cannot be rectified ... unless the root of the problem is tackled. Hence, it is essential to hit the main enemy [the United States] ..."[12]

That the Arab Spring toppled President Hosni Mubarak in Egypt and President Zine El Abidine Ben Ali in Tunisia undermines al-Qaeda's claim that the only viable solution to reform was violently forcing the far enemy to withdraw its support for apostate leaders, thereby making these local regimes vulnerable to attack. Adding insult to injury is the fact that the protesters accomplished in days what AQAM and its predecessors failed to achieve in decades.

Even the very nature of the protests discredited AQAM's call for jihad against the far enemy. Whereas bin Laden and his followers killed and maimed, those who took to the streets protested nonviolently. AQAM's explanation for the problems facing Muslims centered on the hidden power of Western puppeteers, but the protesters focused on local grievances like the lack of jobs, corruption, and ineffective governance. The protesters' motivations were largely secular and modern, while AQAM marched under the banner of religion. Where bin Laden and Zawahiri have called for a pan-Islamic state based on Shari'a, the Arab streets have been calling for true democracy and a voice in shaping the future of their respective nations. The Arab Spring was therefore a withering indictment of bin Laden's far enemy strategy.

> The Arab Spring was a withering indictment of bin Laden's far enemy strategy.

Al-Qaeda core's global conception of "defensive jihad" is the second ideological innovation threatened by the Arab Spring. Bin Laden articulated this idea in his second fatwa against the United States in 1998, stating that killing "Americans and their allies—civilians and military—is an individual duty for every Muslim who can do it in any country in which it is possible to do it."[13] This disturbing statement built upon the various lines of thinking from jihadi ideologues. One such thinker was Muhammad Abdal-Salam Faraj, an Egyptian revolutionary who was executed as a co-conspirator in Sadat's assassination. Faraj posited that jihad against apostate leaders was an individual duty for all Muslims. Another influential figure was Abdullah Azzam, a mentor of bin Laden's, whose calls that Muslims must actively defend Muslim lands from non-Muslim aggression were met internationally with volunteers and donations. This obligation has been built on the underlying narrative that the West is at war with Islam, occupying Muslim lands and taking their resources, and that Western policies are geared toward the degradation and humiliation of Muslims. The global defensive jihad is a reaction to this worldview. If bin Laden's first innovation focused the jihad on the far enemy, his second made it an individual duty for all able Muslims to commit to that fight, regardless of where they reside.

Bin Laden's global formulation of defensive jihad relies on persistent oppression. At the moment protesters took to the streets in control of events and their own lives—freeing Tunisian and Egyptian Muslims from the shackles of dictatorship—the underlying theme of a perpetually victimized Muslim populace evaporated, and defensive jihad on their behalf became pointless. With the United States seemingly playing little role in the unfolding events in the Middle East and allowing its long-time allies in Tunis and Cairo to be ushered out of power, the narrative of the oppressive West rang hollow. Although AQAM's call for defensive jihad may still resonate in the context of pan-Islamist causes related to the perceived occupation of Muslim lands such as Afghanistan and Chechnya, the Arab Spring has made bin Laden's plea virtually irrelevant in places where reform is eroding repression.

With bin Laden's death, there is also a challenge to the cohesion of these ideological underpinnings within the global movement he helped spawn. Though AQAM has been injected with this global jihadi DNA, AQAM will likely have more difficulty maintaining ideological and strategic coherence without bin Laden in place to coalesce the movement.

Not only has bin Laden's demise and the Arab Spring weakened AQAM's ideological underpinnings, this moment has also ushered in hope that the social and political malaise affecting Arab populations can be redressed. These are conditions AQAM has traditionally exploited. It is no coincidence that the nations touched by revolution were characterized by a profound lack of freedom. According to Freedom House, 88 percent of people in the Middle East and North Africa were "not free" in 2010, the highest percentage globally.[14]

Unable to determine their political fate, most Arabs were ruled by longstanding autocrats who had little tolerance for dissent. When these leaders did undertake reforms or participate in elections, as Mubarak did on four separate occasions, the intention was to create the illusion of progress in order to mollify Western audiences and restive constituents. Today, many Arabs are, for the first time in their lives, witnessing freedom and the ability to shape their political destinies. Such jubilation is a far cry from the hopelessness and humiliation that served as AQAM's midwife.

The sense of elation and self-empowerment borne from the Arab Spring cannot be understated. Contrary to what terrorists like Zawahiri may claim,

AQAM played no role: All the credit belongs to the Arabs who took to the streets. Accordingly, AQAM seems even less relevant in MENA than before the protests occurred. After all, what good are a bunch of militants scattered throughout the badlands of Pakistan and Somalia when non-violent Arabs can overturn their governments? Further marginalized in the eyes of their Arab constituents, AQAM's future as the self-appointed vanguard of the global jihad seems fragile and under existential threat.

This assessment rests on a comforting but perhaps misleading assumption, however. What if the aspirations of the protesters are not met and the revolutions do not bring about long-term reform? What if the bitter harvest of the Arab Spring is disillusionment and discontent? In Syria, Yemen, and Bahrain, this could mean raised expectations deflated by the protestors' inability to overturn the status quo. In Egypt, Tunisia, and Libya, where the Arab Spring has displaced the status quo, failure could manifest differently. No longer unified in opposition to the old system, significant disagreements among the protesters could stifle the fragile democratic process. Longstanding traditions of corruption and patronage politics or the rise of a new dictator—secular or theocratic—could have a similar effect in these countries.

> Zawahiri and other AQAM leaders are betting hard that the Arab Spring will implode.

Zawahiri and other AQAM leaders are betting hard that the Arab Spring will implode. As AQIM warned in its message to the people of Tunisia, "... it is the right of the Ummah to celebrate this partial victory. It is also its duty to not miss what is intended against it, and to remain cautious and awake, because all the gains it has achieved in this popular revolution ... are now and in the future exposed to thievery, robbery and manipulation."[15]

The failure of the Arab Spring could produce a profound sense of disappointment among an entire generation of Arabs. Amid this despair, AQAM's message that armed struggle against the West is the only viable path to reform could find fertile ground. Such a development would be a strategic opportunity for AQAM to reassert itself and regain its relevance in MENA.

Even if this scenario does not come to pass and the reforms catalyzed by the protests enjoy broad-based support, it is a virtual certainty that some constituencies will be left unsatisfied. These aggrieved groups or individuals could become vulnerable to AQAM's ideology, and a small subset might even provide passive or active support to the movement. AQAM does not need to take over the entirety of the protest movement or occupy a capital to regain momentum. Though few in number, disillusioned and radicalized individuals could help restore AQAM's relevance within MENA. As the movement's history has shown, a small but dedicated nucleus of adherents can survive robust pressure and have geopolitical impact.

How Might AQAM Respond?

Although AQAM is not the central protagonist in the Arab Spring, it will nonetheless try to manipulate the situation to serve its ends. Its statements after the protests erupted—in particular those from Zawahiri—are a clear indication of the movement's intent to shape the narrative of the Arab Spring as disillusionment likely emerges within Arab populations. The movement's strategic priorities with regard to the Arab Spring are threefold. First, AQAM will see this as an opportunity to take advantage of the security vacuum and chaos resulting from the tumult in Arab countries. Second, it will seek to prevent its principal ideological innovations from fading into irrelevance. Third, it will lay the necessary groundwork to exploit fully the wave of discontent that could arise if the Arab Spring fails to bring about lasting and sufficient reform.

In the first instance, AQAM leaders lauded the overthrow of longstanding autocrats like Mubarak and Ben Ali and called for the attack and overthrow of others like Muammar Qaddafi in Libya. They also have viewed the toppling of authoritarian regimes as an opportunity for greater operational activity. In his essay, "Tsunami of Change," Anwar al-Awlaki noted that "our mujahidin brothers . . . will get a chance to breathe again after three decades of suffocation" and "the great doors of opportunity would open up for the mujahidin all over the world."[16]

More importantly, in its statements AQAM has set forth arguments intended to explain the continued relevance of its two ideological innovations. In fact, Zawahiri has used the revolutions to *reemphasize* the importance of AQAM's campaign against the far enemy. In his third statement to the Egyptian people, Zawahiri argued that the West discarded Ben Ali when his usefulness expired and inserted a new regime that would give the impression of freedom, but in reality continued to serve Western interests.[17] By spinning this conspiratorial tale of the revolution, Zawahiri downplayed the amazing impact of the Tunisian protestors and identified the West as the ultimate arbiter of events in the country. To truly own their destiny, this argument follows, Tunisians—and Muslims more broadly—must remove Western influence.

Zawahiri also keeps the focus on the far enemy by arguing that AQAM's campaign against the West made the revolutions possible in the first place. In his fourth statement to the Egyptians, he claimed that "America's decline and change in its policies to support the titan tyrants, and her attempt to treat the Muslim peoples with policies of flexibility, trickery and soft power, did not happen but as a direct result of the blessed battles in New York and Washington and Pennsylvania ...."[18]

Not only did Zawahiri defend AQAM's far enemy focus to date, but he also promoted its continuation. For Zawahiri, the departure of Mubarak was not enough. Accordingly, he promised that AQAM will "continue attacking America and its partners and aggravate them, until they leave ... Muslim homelands and stop supporting the titan tyrants in them ...."[19] For those who hoped that the Arab Spring might reorient AQAM's leadership away from the West, think again.

Several statements implicitly addressed the erosion of AQAM's second innovation: the universal conception of defensive jihad. AQAM's argument was a simple one: although the removal of Mubarak and Ben Ali were victories, the paramount goal of implementing Shari'a remains unachieved and therefore violent struggle remains obligatory. A communiqué issued by AQIM made this point to the people of Tunisia, stating, "The tyrant has left and the system of tyranny and Kufr (disbelief) remains; you have won a battle but you haven't won the war yet. And here are the Jews, the Crusaders and the apostates plotting against you. Continue your battle to overthrow the tyrannical system ...."[20]

Zawahiri echoed this notion in his fourth statement to Egyptians: "the honorable, free ones who are protective over their religion ... must not be satisfied with removing the tyrant ... but also they have to continue Jihad and resistance until the Islamic regime rises, which would achieve justice, freedom, and independence."[21] As far as AQAM is concerned, regardless of whether or not political activism bears fruit, jihad will continue to be an individual obligation for all Muslims until the entire Muslim-majority world resembles the now defunct Islamic Emirate of Afghanistan.

In his only statement to have emerged on the Arab Spring, bin Laden cautioned against losing the "historic opportunity to raise the Ummah and be liberated from enslavement to the wishes of the rulers and the man-made laws for Western domination."[22] Interestingly, though, he made no attempt to defend his two ideological innovations, putting him oddly out of synch with other AQAM spokesmen. He made no exhortations for violent resistance nor did he focus on the far enemy.

Regardless of this particular message, AQAM's leaders have clearly made it a priority to defend their ideology from the Arab Spring. Having done so, AQAM will also try to leverage whatever discontent may arise as the political process plays out. This opportunistic strategy is not new. In the run-up to the U.S. invasion of Iraq, bin Laden and other AQAM figures effectively positioned the movement to leverage the significant wave of anger that resulted from the invasion of a second Muslim country by U.S. forces. Initially this strategy was successful, and AQI was able to use outrage to attract a consistent flow of foreign fighters from outside of Iraq.

Certainly, if disillusionment makes the environment more receptive to AQAM's ideology, the movement will find recruits, funding, and logistical support to operate and grow. Greater leeway to operate would not only mean the likelihood of more terrorism and sectarian violence, but also greater acceptance and embedding of the underlying principles of AQAM's ideology, which run counter to the precepts of democracy and individual rights and liberties.

AQAM strategists will take advantage of the environment that will emerge—whether it is leveraging greater operational breathing space or feeding off the disillusionment of the protesters—to rebuild support for its ideology. Their statements and resulting narrative will attempt to shape expectations and the perceptions of the people of the Arab world, especially those who may not be convinced that the Arab Spring can bring real change. They will also use any steps—missteps or otherwise—taken by the United States to their advantage. The challenge for AQAM to remain relevant takes on greater significance with the death of bin Laden, with its leadership and survival as an organization at risk.

How Might AQAM Change?

Importantly though, AQAM and its ideology will not remain immune from the effects of the ever-changing landscape of this new Middle East. The shifting environment and the circumstances in each country will affect the movement's trajectory. These changes—directed or organic—may be accelerated because of the leadership crisis and internal divisions arising in the wake of bin Laden's death. There are interesting possibilities in anticipating AQAM's adaptations.

First, AQAM may need to address more directly the opening of political space in Arab countries, particularly the expanding role of Islamist groups in politics. We have seen this debate play out in al-Qaeda core's consistent criticism of Hamas for engaging in political activities to the detriment of jihad on behalf of the Palestinian people. This conflict manifests itself in statements lobbed between the groups, but it has played out on the ground in Gaza, where al-Qaeda-inspired Salafi jihadi groups have challenged Hamas and created headaches for the Hamas leadership.[23] Thus, a more open political environment will present AQAM with the challenge of maintaining its importance when Islamist movements are carrying the banner of Shari'a and Islam through civic and political engagement.

In the current, fluid environment, it would be unwise to dismiss the possibility that segments of AQAM may alter their modus operandi—accelerating strategic debates already present within the movement on the eve of the Arab Spring. Faced with mounting internal pressures before the protests even began, AQAM's leaders have already hinted at some potentially new approaches.

One possibility is an attempt by AQAM to reduce the number of attacks against Muslim civilians, thereby buttressing its popularity and avoiding the mistakes that contributed to its defeat in Iraq and its subsequent loss of legitimacy in MENA. An al-Qaeda core figure named Shaykh Atiyallah called for such an adjustment in a March 2011 statement, urging commanders to issue orders "forbidding bombings and … massacres at Muslim mosques and their surroundings, and public places such as markets, stadiums …… regardless of what the goal may be."[24] Such a shift in tactics would parallel statements made by other jihadi leaders that attacks on Muslim civilians are often regrettable mistakes. Zawahiri set forth this theme of tempering violence and restricting battles in his 2005 letter of admonition to Abu Musab al-Zarqawi in Iraq, warning him to learn from the mistakes of the Taliban to avoid alienating the local population.[25]

A focus on development as a tool for the movement could be another potential shift for AQAM. A wide variety of terrorist organizations—including entities within AQAM's orbit such as Lashkar-e-Taiba (LeT)—have successfully leveraged social welfare programs to boost their support base and fundraising. Groups like Hamas and Hezbollah have demonstrated that terrorist organizations can profit handsomely and build loyalty from established charitable operations.

These lessons are not lost on al-Qaeda's core. In the wake of the 2010 floods that decimated Pakistan, bin Laden issued a statement focusing heavily on the need to ensure relief for the Pakistani people and called for the provision of aid and the creation of a "capable relief task force that has the knowledge and experience needed."[26] In his final speech, bin Laden also advocated the establishment of a "council that provides opinions and advice to the Muslim people" in order to help protect revolutions that have taken place, advance those in progress, and launch new ones.[27] Although many dismiss these statements as poorly conceived attempts to repair his damaged reputation, bin Laden's focused comments on the need for organized aid and assistance efforts suggest that he understood the benefits that accrue from helping people meet their material needs. Following the Pakistan earthquakes in 2005, Zawahiri also made pleas for relief to those affected, criticizing the United States for its purported assault on Islamic charities.

Although there is a major gap between these statements and a wholesale strategic shift, the mere mention of avoiding Muslim casualties and providing social services suggests that AQAM's leadership has recognized alternatives to its current approach and opens the possibility that segments of the movement could adapt to use these tools. If implemented, such changes could help the movement repair its tarnished image in MENA, better positioning it to regain relevance should the Arab Spring fail to deliver.

Given the degree of AQAM's decentralization, however, it seems unlikely that AQAM's leadership after bin Laden could reorient the movement even if they made that decision. If AQAM's leadership were to issue top-down directives calling for a significant strategic shift in response to the Arab Spring, it would more than likely lead to further fragmentation of the broader movement and its ideology. In addition, al-Qaeda core continues to see itself as the violent vanguard of the Muslim community and could view the work of charities as important but the province of other Islamist groups.

AQAM has already begun to shape its own narrative in the context of the Arab Spring. The environment will be fluid and no doubt affect AQAM's strategies, but it will surely take advantage of opportunities presented to reassert itself in the heart of its constituency and to prove its ongoing relevance. In this regard, it is banking on discontent and disillusionment to follow the Arab Spring.

Impact of the Arab Spring on U.S. efforts to combat AQAM

Since September 11, 2001, the United States has led a global campaign against AQAM. This offensive has relied not just on enhanced U.S. counterterrorism capabilities but on local allies to pressure and dismantle AQAM operations and networks. Many of the regimes weakened or deposed by the Arab Spring were among Washington's most effective counterterrorism partners. The erosion or wholesale collapse of these governments creates a host of new counterterrorism challenges for the United States, as do other developments caused by the Arab Spring.

In the near term, the Arab Spring has interrupted operational pressure on AQAM. Egypt and Tunisia have both disbanded their reviled state security agencies, disrupting the structures that kept tabs on jihadists (and non-violent political dissidents).[28] Both countries also freed scores of political prisoners, among them Islamists and jihadists. In Yemen, reports indicate that President Ali Abdullah Saleh has redeployed forces pursuing AQAP to the capital to preserve his rule, prompting U.S. policymakers to consider unilateral counterterrorism activities in the country.[29] Swaths of Libya are entirely outside of government control, providing openings for AQIM and any violent remnants of LIFG.

This does not mean to imply that full-blown safe havens have emerged throughout MENA. The caretaker governments in Egypt and Tunisia and the Yemeni protesters do not appear to welcome AQAM. Nevertheless, the political upheaval has shifted priorities away from AQAM, creating new space for the movement to operate where none existed before. Caught between uncommitted or distracted governments and aware of the negative fallout that would result from unconstrained, unilateral counterterrorism operations, the United States is limited in what it can do. It can continue to press governments to maintain pressure on known AQAM figures and networks, ensure it maintains relationships with security service personnel who will be important to counterterrorism cooperation, and attempt to coalesce more focused regional coalitions to pressure the movement. This could be a model applied with Saudi Arabia and the United Arab Emirates to ensure AQAP does not gain breathing space in Yemen.

In addition to weakening counterterrorism pressure, the Arab Spring may be creating a more ideologically permissive environment for AQAM. Prior to the unrest, repressive governments prevented hardline ideologues from openly espousing their beliefs. Although this policy constrained freedom of expression and therefore had its disadvantages, it kept AQAM on the ideological fringes. With the opening created by the Arab Spring, public discourse in several countries has shifted, allowing some influential individuals to call publicly for certain actions or outcomes consonant with AQAM's ideology.

> The Arab Spring may be creating a more ideologically permissive environment for AQAM.

In February 2011, for instance, Abdul Majid al-Zindani, a Yemeni cleric who is labeled by the U.S. Treasury as a specially designated global terrorist and "carries considerable political and moral weight," called for the removal of the Saleh regime and its replacement with an Islamic state.[30] In Egypt, the triumphal return of Yusuf al-Qaradawi, the charismatic voice of the Muslim Brotherhood, may give greater legitimacy to the use of suicide bombings against "oppressors and occupiers," which he advocates and has condoned. Even though Qaradawi and AQAM are not directly linked, the open promotion of suicide attacks, as justified by a recognized religious leader and authorized under Islamic precepts, could open the dialogue for AQAM's defensive jihad principles. In the context of such statements, AQAM's violent jihad may seem more legitimate in the public eye.

Another immediate counterterrorism challenge posed by the Arab Spring is the conflict in Libya. This confrontation plays to AQAM's favor for several reasons. Libya's northeast has a history of radicalization, and the fighting there seems to have mobilized local jihadists.[31] If the conflict becomes protracted, Libya could begin to attract foreign volunteers—perhaps using the same infrastructure that AQIM used to funnel North Africans to Iraq. The migration of foreign fighters to Libya would create a new network of Arab jihadists with combat experience. Another concern is that individuals linked with AQAM could access and export weapons used by rebel forces. Of particular concern are man-portable air-defense systems (MANPADS), which AQAM has used with varying degrees of success to target aircraft from Kenya to Afghanistan. An unnamed Algerian security official quoted by Reuters claimed that AQIM had already managed to obtain a consignment of SA-7 missiles and smuggle them into northern Mali.[32]

> The conflict in Libya plays to al-Qaeda's favor for several reasons.

If inadequate reform leads to disillusionment, the Arab Spring could boost AQAM's resonance in MENA and ultimately produce a new set of long-term counterterrorism challenges for the United States and its Western partners. Even if the reformers somehow manage to fully eradicate the old guard, overcome cultures of corruption, and implement legitimate and effective governance, they will still need to address demographic pressures, economic challenges, high unemployment, and increasing resource constraints. In short, the challenges facing the Arab world are so myriad and severe that some degree of alienation seems unavoidable.

AQAM will do everything it can to exploit this discontent—even if takes years to do so. Whether its efforts will ultimately succeed is an open question. If the movement manages to position itself as a viable alternative to an ineffective political process, AQAM will likely enjoy increased popular support, additional recruits, and more donors. All of this could lead to a renewed AQAM threat in the Arab world, only this time the United States may not have effective local partners.

It is unclear right now how the Arab Spring will ultimately impact the underlying AQAM narrative of the West being at war with Islam. There is no question though that if the United States is seen to have abandoned the courageous activists fighting for liberty and democracy, it would reinforce this notion—this time drawing on the disillusionment of democrats and dissidents.

It is also unclear how the events in the Arab world will impact the growing allure of AQAM's Siren Song in the West. The trend of radicalization in the West seems to be driven more by local factors such as sub-communal identities (as seen in the radicalization of some Somali–American youth), assimilation and identity issues in Europe, and reactions to U.S. and European counterterrorism and foreign policies.[33] These issues and perceptions by radicalized Westerners may be unaffected by the street protests and the spirit of the Arab Spring.

That said, if AQAM and its ideology are dealt a severe blow in the heart of the Sunni Arab world, the global movement may not be able to recover, and its appeal will grow weaker over time, even if adherents to the cause continue to cause problems. It is not yet clear what the loss of bin Laden will do to the allure of AQAM and its ideology in the West. It is certainly possible that the death of the recognizable leader of the global jihad could diminish the heroic appeal of the movement over time to those who have yet to be radicalized.

A Strategic Moment for U.S. Counterterrorism Policies

Despite these complications, the Arab Spring also represents a significant opportunity for U.S. counterterrorism efforts. This is a strategic moment for the United States because, for the first time, Washington's values, long-term interests, and counterterrorism goals against AQAM neatly align with events in the region. The Arab Spring represents what U.S. policymakers have argued and hoped for in countering AQAM's ideology—organic movements for democracy, individual rights, and liberties in the heart of its Sunni Arab constituency. This strategic window is further helped by the killing of bin Laden, an action that will keep al-Qaeda core's leadership on its heels and will roil an AQAM that relied on bin Laden for symbolic and strategic direction and cohesion.

The critical question then becomes what to do to seize this moment without tainting the organic movements for reform. Aside from maintaining operational pressure on AQAM however possible and preventing successful attacks, the United States and Western allies cannot be passive about the long-term counterterrorism implications of the Arab Spring. The Obama administration needs to recognize this strategic opportunity and realize that the battle for reform in the Arab world could lead to AQAM's demise or pave the path for its return.

> Washington cannot be shy about shaping the reform that is already underway.

Washington cannot be shy about shaping the reform that is already underway. Where autocrats have been toppled (as in Tunisia and Egypt), the United States needs to help shape the post-autocratic environment; with non-democratic, allied regimes (as with the region's monarchies), it needs to help accelerate internal, non-violent reform; and with repressive regimes that are antithetical to U.S. interests (like Syria and Iran), Washington needs to question their legitimacy and push for regime change while assisting protesters.

This is not a call for further military intervention or the imposition of American-style democracy in the Arab world. Instead, the United States should use its significant influence against AQAM by engaging in an all-out effort to support economic and political reform in the Middle East and North Africa. This will require a focused campaign, with the United States setting the framework and then enlisting state and non-state allies to support the spirit of the Arab Spring.[34]

Some have argued for a new Marshall Plan for the region. The focus of such an effort would be right, but in a resource-constrained environment, this may not be realistic. In lieu of direct nation-building on a massive scale, the United States should consider a society-wide effort that takes advantage of America's strategic suasion and leverages the diffusion of power and influence to support the organic movements in the region. This could be a 21st-century Marshall Plan, with resources and leverage consolidated from state and non-state sources. Aspects of this initiative could include:

- Democracy and election advocates—enabled by the U.S. Agency for International Development (USAID)—could help civil society grow and newly-organized groups establish grassroots political prowess.

- As called for by democracy advocate Natan Sharansky,[35] special focus and funding, buttressed by human rights groups, could organize and empower the networks of democracy dissidents throughout the Arab world.

- Women's advocacy groups and trade unions could support the strengthening of counterpart organizations throughout the Middle East.

- Deep-pocket philanthropists and America's diverse and powerful diaspora business communities could drive new investments, entrepreneurship initiatives, and economic opportunities for the youth of the region.

- Technology and Internet companies interested in open communications (and customers) could help expand the reach of communication tools, in part to aid political mobilization, but also government accountability and transparency.

- Along with technical assistance, anti-corruption advocates and organizations like Transparency International could help bring best practices for governmental transparency and electronic banking practices to combat corruption.

- Academic institutions like Harvard University, collections of scientists, and academics could serve as detached incubators and conveners for conflict resolution and novel political solutions where crisis persists in the region.

- Hollywood and Bollywood writers and producers could begin collaboration to lionize the new heroes of the Middle East—the non-violent democracy activists who bravely took to the streets and are working for a new future.

Though the United States needs to be careful not to be the central protagonist or taint the organic movements of the Arab Spring—thereby playing into Zawahiri's narrative of the United States being the grand puppeteer—it cannot sit idly by hoping that all works out for the best. With likely disillusionment on the horizon, the time to shape the reform is now.

President Obama's May speech certainly set forth the outlines for U.S. involvement and values and offered explicit and actionable measures to bolster the Egyptian and Tunisian economies, among other objectives. This, along with a follow-up commitment from the G8 economies for an initial pledge of at least $20 billion in assistance to Egypt and Tunisia, are important signals and steps, but they are not sufficient to sustain the type of reform needed. Absent in persistent attention, these measures will not suffice if the United States hopes to be an indispensible partner for Arab reformers and in so doing irrevocably diminish AQAM's prospects in the Arab world. Achieving these objectives will require the fulfillment of our commitments, sustained focus, and, importantly, a society-wide effort to leverage the unique expertise and influence of private citizens, non-governmental organizations, and corporations.

Admittedly, in many quarters, the United States has not been seen as a consistent or credible advocate for democracy in the Arab world. Its longstanding deals and relationships with autocratic regimes and the region's monarchies cast shadows on the ideals of American democracy. This moment, however, provides an opportunity for a strategic adjustment and recalibration of perceptions. The principles of the Arab Spring—rooted in individual liberties and the shedding of fear and oppression—are fundamentally American principles for which the United States and its people are best suited to support and advocate.

Importantly, this approach would help bring clarity to the broader U.S. policy toward the Arab Spring and the region. The approach would be the right policy overall to ensure the aspirations of those who have courageously taken to the streets. It would align with U.S. values and interests. Importantly, too, it would help answer the challenge from AQAM to define what happens next and would further ensure that the movement remains on its heels after the death of bin Laden. If the United States makes a significant effort to help the Arab Spring succeed in the long term, it will accelerate the defeat of AQAM and its ideology. Combined with the killing of bin Laden, this could mark the beginning of the end of the long war.

Notes

1. Laura Mansfield, *His Own Words: A Translation of the Writings of Dr. Ayman Al Zawahiri* (TLG Publications, 2006), p. 247–248.
2. See, for example, Fareed Zakaria, "Fareed's Take: Al Qaeda is irrelevant," CNN, March 7, 2011, http://globalpublicsquare.blogs.cnn.com/2011/03/07/al-qaeda-is-irrelevant/.
3. Juan C. Zarate, "Al Qaeda Stirs Again," *New York Times*, April 17, 2011, http://www.nytimes.com/2011/04/18/opinion/18Zarate.html.
4. Juan Zarate, "Al Qaeda's Divisions Within," *New York Times*, May 2, 2011, http://www.nytimes.com/roomfordebate/2011/05/02/the-war-on-terror-after-osama-bin-laden/al-qaedas-internal-divisions.

5. Daniel Kimmage, "Al-Qaeda Central and the Internet," New America Foundation, March 2010, p. 4, http://counterterrorism.newamerica.net/sites/newamerica.net/files/policydocs/kimmage2_0.pdf.

6. Ibid.

7. Peter Bergen, *The Longest War: The Enduring Conflict Between America and Al-Qaeda* (Free Press, 2011), p. 267.

8. National Counterterrorism Center, "Al-Qa'ida in Iraq (AQI)," http://www.nctc.gov/site/groups/aqi.html.

9. National Counterterrorism Center, "Al-Qa'ida in the Lands of the Islamic Maghreb (AQIM)," http://www.nctc.gov/site/groups/aqim.html.

10. "Exploiting Grievances: Al-Qaeda in the Arabian Peninsula–Executive Summary," Carnegie Endowment for International Peace, http://www.carnegieendowment.org/files/AQAP_Exploiting_Grievances_Executive_Summary.pdf.

11. Mansfield, p. 209.

12. Osama bin Laden, "Declaration of War against the Americans Occupying the Land of the Two Holy Places," August 1996, http://www.pbs.org/newshour/terrorism/international/fatwa_1996.html.

13. Osama bin Laden, Ayman al-Zawahiri et al., "Second Fatwa," February 23, 1998, http://www.pbs.org/newshour/terrorism/international/fatwa_1998.html.

14. Freedom House, "Freedom in the World 2011: The Authoritarian Challenge to Democracy," http://www.freedomhouse.org/images/File/fiw/Tables%2C%20Graphs%2C%20etc%2C%20FIW%202011_Revised%201_11_11.pdf.

15. "Al-Qaida in the Islamic Maghreb: To Our People in Tunisia," January 26, 2011, http://www.globalterroralert.com/images/documents/pdf/1210/flashpoint_aqimtunisia0111-2.pdf.

16. Anwar al-Awlaki, "The Tsunami of Change," Al-Qaeda in the Arabian Peninsula's *Inspire* Magazine, March 29, 2011, http://www.globalterroralert.com/images/documents/pdf/1210/flashpoint_inspire032911awlaki.pdf.

17. Ayman al-Zawahiri, "Message of Hope and Glad Tidings to Our People in Egypt, Episode 3," February 27, 2011, http://www.globalterroralert.com/images/documents/pdf/1210/flashpoint_zawahiri0227.pdf.

18. Ayman al-Zawahiri, "Message of Hope and Glad Tidings to Our People in Egypt, Episode 4," March 3, 2011, http://www.globalterroralert.com/images/documents/pdf/1210/flashpoint_zawahiri030311.pdf.

19. Ibid.

20. "Al-Qaida in the Islamic Maghreb: To Our People in Tunisia."

21. Zawahiri, "Message of Hope and Glad Tidings to Our People in Egypt, Episode 4."

22. Usama bin Laden, "Message to His Ummah," May 18, 2011, http://www.globalterroralert.com/images/documents/pdf/0110/flashpoint_ublfinal0511.pdf.

23. Yoram Cohen and Matthew Levitt, with Becca Wasser, "Deterred but Determined: Salafi-Jihadi Groups in the Palestinian Arena," The Washington Institute for Near East Policy, Policy Focus #99, January 2010, http://www.washingtoninstitute.org/pubPDFs/PolicyFocus%2099.pdf.

24. Shaykh Atiyallah, "Glorifying the Sanctity of the Muslims' Blood," March 14, 2011, http://www.globalterroralert.com/images/documents/pdf/1210/flashpoint_atiyallah031411.pdf.

25. "Zawahiri's Letter to Zarqawi," Combating Terrorism Center at West Point, July 9, 2005, http://www.ctc.usma.edu/posts/zawahiris-letter-to-zaraqawi-english-translation.

26. "Bin Laden addresses climate change," Al Jazeera, October 1, 2010, http://english.aljazeera.net/news/asia/2010/10/201010115560631340.html.

27. Usama bin Laden, "Message to His Ummah."

28. "Tunisia dissolves its state security division," CNN, March 7, 2011, http://articles.cnn.com/2011-03-07/world/tunisia.state.security_1_fouad-mebazaa-tunis-afrique-presse-president-zine-el?_s=PM:WORLD; Zeina Karam, "Egypt Dissolves Hated State Security Agency," Associated Press, March 15, 2011, http://abcnews.go.com/International/wireStory?id=13140119.

29. Dina Temple-Raston, "Trouble in Yemen Could Give Al-Qaida New Opening," NPR, April 6, 2011, http://www.npr.org/2011/04/06/135157516/trouble-in-yemen-could-give-al-qaida-new-opening.

30. Laura Kasinof and Scott Shane, "Radical Cleric Demands Ouster of Yemen Leader," New York Times, March 1, 2011, http://www.nytimes.com/2011/03/02/world/middleeast/02yemen.html.

31. According to a captured roster of foreign fighters in Iraq, there were more Libyans per capita than any other country. Of these Libyans, 60.2 percent came from Darnah and 23.9 percent came from Benghazi. See, "Al-Qa'ida's Foreign Fighters in Iraq: A First Look at the Sinjar Records," Combating Terrorism Center at West Point, December 2007, pp. 11–12, http://tarpley.net/docs/CTCForeignFighter.19.Dec07.pdf.

32. Lamine Chikhi, "Al Qaeda acquiring weapons in Libya: Algerian official," Reuters, April 4, 2011, http://af.reuters.com/article/topNews/idAFJOE7330LB20110404.

33. See, Marc Sageman, Leaderless Jihad: Terror Networks in the Twenty-First Century (Philadelphia: University of Pennsylvania Press, 2008), especially Chapter 4 "Radicalization in the Diaspora."

34. Zarate, "Al Qaeda Stirs Again."

35. Natan Sharansky, "Why I'm hopeful about the Middle East uprisings," Washington Post, March 11, 2011, http://www.washingtonpost.com/opinions/amid-the-mideast-uprisings-an-opening-for-democracy/2011/03/10/ABgPPTR_story.html.

Daniel Byman

Israel's Pessimistic View of the Arab Spring

Americans took heart as they watched Egyptian demonstrators rally in Tahrir Square and topple the regime of Hosni Mubarak in a peaceful revolution. Next door in Israel, however, the mood was somber: "When some people in the West see what's happening in Egypt, they see Europe 1989," an Israeli official remarked. "We see it as Tehran 1979."[1] Political leaders vied to see who could be the most pessimistic, with Israeli Prime Minister Benjamin Netanyahu publicly warning that it was even possible that "Egypt will go in the direction of Iran," with the new Cairo government becoming even more dictatorial and lashing out abroad.[2] As he pointed out in remarks to the Knesset, "They too had demonstrations; multitudes filled the town squares. But, of course it progressed in a different way."[3] As unrest spread from Egypt to Bahrain, Jordan, Syria, and Yemen, the gloom seemed to deepen.

These apocalyptic predictions and Israel's doom-and-gloom mentality are easy, too easy, to dismiss. Israelis are always sensitive to their security. Indeed, their reaction to the spread of democracy so close to their borders seems churlish, as does their tendency to look on the dark side when so many of their Arab neighbors now have hopes for a better life. But dismissing Israeli concerns would be a mistake. Some of Israel's fears are valid, and others that are less so will still drive Israeli policies. The new regimes and the chaotic regional situation pose security challenges to the Jewish state. These challenges, and the Israeli reactions to them, are likely to worsen the crisis in Gaza and make the prospects for peace between the Israelis and Palestinians even more remote. The

Daniel Byman is a Professor in the Security Studies Program at Georgetown University and the Research Director of the Saban Center for Middle East Policy at Brookings. He is also the author of A High Price: The Triumphs and Failures of Israeli Counterterrorism (Oxford University Press, 2011) and an editorial board member for TWQ. He can be reached at dlb32@georgetown.edu.

Copyright © 2011 Center for Strategic and International Studies
The Washington Quarterly • 34:3 pp. 123–136
DOI: 10.1080/0163660X.2011.588139

Dismissing Israeli concerns would be a mistake.

new revolutions also have the potential to complicate the U.S.–Israel relationship further and make it harder for the United States to benefit from the Arab Spring.

In the end, however, neither the United States nor Israel is behind the winds of change sweeping the Middle East. Egypt will have a new regime, and other Arab countries may too. Others may reform, while still others may become more reactionary, or even, as in Libya, collapse into civil war. Decrying this trend risks missing opportunities to nudge it in the right direction. It is in Israel's interest, as well as Washington's, that the regional transformation is peaceful and that democratization succeeds.

Fear Factors

The list of Israeli concerns about the wave of revolution sweeping the Arab world is long. Some concerns are overstated or erroneous, but others are understandable and legitimate. And because both the irrational and rational concerns will drive Israeli policy, all deserve serious attention.

When Friends Become Enemies

The biggest Israeli concern, and the one that has gotten the most attention, is the replacement of the Mubarak regime in Egypt by, well, that's the question. For much of Israel's history, Egypt was its most dangerous foe, and the two countries fought bitter wars in 1948, 1956, 1967, 1969–1970, and 1973. Egyptian President Anwar Sadat upended this seemingly constant belligerency when he made peace with Israel, transforming Israel's greatest foe into a partner. Islamist extremists killed Sadat, in part because of his embrace of peace, and Israelis still honor his memory. Mubarak never won the goodwill of ordinary Israelis as did Sadat or the late King Hussein of Jordan, but he did maintain the peace treaty, cooperate on counterterrorism, oppose Iran, and otherwise share strategic objectives with the Jewish state. And he and his regime seemed immovable. Israeli analyst Aluf Benn points out that "Israel has replaced eight prime ministers, fought several wars, and engaged in peace talks with multiple partners, and Mubarak was always there."[4]

Who comes to power next is of tremendous concern to Israel. Netanyahu and others are particularly fearful that Islamists, led by the Muslim Brotherhood, will gain power, either legitimately through democratic elections or by seizing power during a time of chaos. The Brotherhood often criticized Sadat and then Mubarak for making peace with Israel, pointing to this as one (of many) factors that de-legitimized the regime. In February, days before Mubarak stepped down,

Rashad al-Bayoumi, a Brotherhood leader, declared, "after President Mubarak steps down and a provisional government is formed, there is a need to dissolve the peace treaty with Israel."[5] Yossi Klein Halevi, an Israeli analyst, points out that a Muslim Brotherhood victory "would bring to power an anti-Semitic movement that is committed to ending Egypt's peace treaty with the Jewish state."[6] Barry Rubin, another Israeli analyst, even warns that Egypt could once again embrace radical nationalism and renew its alliance with Syria.[7]

> Israel is particularly fearful that Islamists, led by the Muslim Brotherhood, will gain power in Egypt.

The Brotherhood's prospects for power are unclear. It enjoys support from many Egyptians, but does not appear to command the loyalty of a majority. Some estimates put Brotherhood support at around 20 percent of the Egyptian population, but this is more guess than science. However, no rival group enjoys support from a majority of Egyptians. In addition, the Brotherhood is well-organized and could gain power simply because secular rivals do not get their electoral act together.

The Brotherhood rejected violence under Mubarak, though Israeli skeptics would say that this was a move driven by necessity given Egypt's powerful security forces, not conviction that violence is wrong. For now, the Brotherhood has stressed that it favors democracy and seeks to work with, not supplant, other Egyptian political forces. The Brotherhood has even declared that it will not run a candidate for president in order to allay concerns in Egypt as well as abroad about its power. But the Brotherhood's organization and power base will make it an important factor in determining Egyptian policy in the years to come.

Hamas' history is rooted in the Muslim Brotherhood, making Israel even more leery of a Brotherhood-influenced regime in Egypt. Hamas has shot at Israeli soldiers and civilians, and launched rockets at and sent suicide bombers into Israeli cities. A like-minded regime in far more powerful Egypt makes Israelis shudder.

Israel's bigger problem is that the Brotherhood is not alone in its anti-Israel sentiment. Israelis focused less on the many Tahrir Square demonstrators whose uplifting pleas for liberty inspired Arabs throughout the region and more on the few who also hanged a puppet with a Star of David on it to symbolize Mubarak while chanting "God Is Great."[8] Even moderate Egyptian leaders who enjoy support in Washington, such as Ayman Nour and Nobel Laureate Mohamed ElBaradei, have called for revising the peace treaty with Israel or holding a referendum on it. Amr Moussa, formerly Egypt's foreign minister and now a leading presidential candidate, has long criticized Israel. He enjoys the distinction of being mentioned in a top pop song, with the lyrics declaring, "I hate Israel and I love Amr Moussa."[9] Nour even declared, "the era of Camp David is over" though he claims to favor revising, not abrogating, the treaty.[10]

It is easy to dismiss statements like Nour's as empty posturing during a lead up to elections. And, more encouragingly, Brotherhood leaders have also made statements to the effect that what is signed is signed—they oppose the peace treaty with Israel, but won't do anything to change it. So, much of the anti-Israel rhetoric is likely to be honored in the breach. However, in a true democracy, politicians cannot always escape their campaign promises. As former U.S. peace negotiator Aaron David Miller contends, "The irony is that the challenges a new Egypt will pose to America and Israel won't come from the worst case scenarios imagined by frantic policymakers and intelligence analysts—an extremist Muslim takeover, an abrogation of peace treaties, the closing of the Suez Canal—but from the very values of participatory government and free speech that free societies so cherish."[11] Anti-Israel sentiment is strong in Egypt. A Pew poll taken after Mubarak's fall found that Egyptians favored annulling the peace treaty with Israel by a 54 percent to 36 percent margin.[12] Leaders who do not make good on promises to distance Egypt from Israel will face criticism and punishment at the polls, particularly if a conflict in Gaza or another crisis again dominates the headlines.

To be clear, no Egyptian government is likely to abrogate the peace treaty with Israel in the near term, and there are few signs of a radical realignment of Egyptian foreign policy. Leading Israeli security officials such as former defense minister Moshe Arens and former Mossad chief Efraim Halevy point out that Egypt's economy is weak and its military depends on the United States. Should Egypt become more bellicose, it would jeopardize the more than $1 billion it gets from Washington every year. Even more important, both foreign investment and tourism would plunge, wreaking havoc on the Egyptian economy. Should Egypt turn to war, the formidable Israel Defense Forces (IDF) would quickly destroy Egyptian forces.[13]

Most Egyptian elites recognize this and accept the necessity of peace, even though they oppose Israeli policies, and many do not accept the legitimacy of the Jewish state. The peace has endured for more than 30 years, and Egypt's current elites, particularly those in the still-influential military, want it to continue because they know a return to war would be disastrous. As Moroccan political scientist Mohamed Darif simply states, "Israel is a fact."[14] Israelis, however, take little comfort that cold calculation will keep the peace going. Their intelligence services did not anticipate Mubarak's fall or other revolts, and they worry that assurances like Darif's will fall by the wayside as the tumult overturns all the certainties of past decades.

Because the peace treaty is likely to endure, it is easy to dismiss Israeli fears regarding Egypt entirely without acknowledging that some Israeli worries are valid. The Egyptian peace with Israel, always cold, could become even chillier. Mubarak, supposedly Israel's friend, only visited Israel once—for the funeral of assassinated Israeli prime minister Yitzhak Rabin—and even then declared "this is not a visit."[15] Intelligence cooperation, pressure on other Arab states to embrace peace initiatives, and (as discussed further below) help for Israel in containing Hamas all may diminish. Egypt has already made overtures to Iran, which Israel considers its nemesis. Egypt allowed an Iranian warship to transit the Suez Canal, and on March 29 acting Egyptian Foreign Minister Nabil al-Arabi announced Egypt would eventually normalize relations with Iran and its Lebanese ally Hezbollah.

Egypt—the largest and most important Arab country, as well as Israel's neighbor—understandably dominates the headlines, but Israelis also worry about other allies. Jordan, which has also signed a peace treaty with Israel and cooperates closely on intelligence matters, is of particular concern. Jordan has been especially helpful to Israel on stopping infiltration into the West Bank and otherwise assisting Israeli counterterrorism. King Abdullah, like his father King Hussein before him, is a staunch friend of Israel. However, he rules over a restive, Palestinian-majority population, and his openly pro-Western and pro-Israeli stance is not popular among his own people. Demonstrations have shaken Jordan, and a government of and by the people there—again, with possible Muslim Brotherhood leadership and a greater Palestinian voice—also raises Israeli fears that another longstanding ally could become hostile almost overnight.

Palestinians, both moderate and militant, are also vulnerable to unrest, and Israelis fear change will create instability and bolster extremists. Both the Hamas government of Gaza and the Fatah-led West Bank have seen unrest. Some Palestinians depict President Mahmoud Abbas, whose moderation regarding Israel makes him so prized in Washington, as a Mubarak clone. The Palestinian Authority government of the West Bank under Abbas' leadership is highly authoritarian—"moderation" applies to his attitude toward Israel, not civil liberties at home. And sure enough, Abbas reacted to unrest in Mubarak style, banning demonstrations and even censoring a television program that mocked Libyan dictator Muammar Qaddafi.[16] While Israelis often scorn, belittle, or ignore Abbas, they also recognize that he is willing to make peace and, perhaps more importantly to many Israelis, crush Hamas and other enemies of Israel on the territory he controls. A new Palestinian leader may not be so conciliatory. Hamas, usually more deft with Palestinian public opinion, was even more heavy handed against the protesters than was Abbas.

To offset pressure for democratic change, Hamas and Abbas' government did the unthinkable: they united, at least on paper. In April, the two signed a unity agreement that would satisfy Palestinians' long-standing demand to end the division created after Hamas and Fatah came to blows in 2007 and Hamas seized power in Gaza. In so doing, both parties could please constituents on a key issue without risking their own holds on power.

Whether this unity lasts is an open question, but Israelis have reacted harshly to it. Many observers in the United States believe Palestinian unity is necessary for peace: Abbas now claims he can negotiate on behalf of all Palestinians, and if Hamas uses terrorism against Israel it risks disrupting inter-Palestinian peace as well as provoking an Israeli reaction. Nevertheless, on May 3, Netanyahu called on Abbas to cancel the agreement, contending that Israel could not make peace with a Palestinian government that included a terrorist organization.

Devils You Know

One of the most surprising Israeli reactions is the apparent concern that unrest could topple adversaries like Bashar al-Assad in Syria. Assad supports Hamas and Hezbollah, rejects peace (or at least has not embraced negotiations, as has Abbas), and is a close friend of Iran. In 2007, Israel even bombed Syria to destroy a suspected nuclear facility there. Assad's regime, however, is less erratic than what came before.

Salah Jadid, the predecessor to Bashar al-Assad's father Hafez, whipped up popular sentiment against Israel, agitating on behalf of the Palestinians to the point that the situation spiraled into war in 1967—a conflict that Damascus was not prepared to fight and resulted in the loss of the Golan Heights to Israel. Hafez, who consolidated power in 1970, learned his lesson and controlled and manipulated popular sentiment, and at times went against it, to avoid a conflict with Israel. His son Bashar takes more risks, but he too recognizes that an open clash with Israel would be disastrous for Syria and his regime.

> The most surprising Israeli reaction may be the apparent concern that unrest could topple Syria.

Relations between Syria and Israel are governed by many rules, most of which are unspoken but are nevertheless quite real. So while Syria supports Hamas, it also places limits on the Palestinian group's activities. In Lebanon, Syria backs the anti-Israel Hezbollah, but also checks its activities when Damascus fears escalation. Changes in Syria could bring to power a new government that does not know these subtle rules and, again, plays to popular opinion rather than strategic reality.

Nor must Assad or other regimes fall for these effects to be felt. Regimes that survive the wave of unrest are likely to be battered in the process. Even if Assad stays in power, he may feel compelled to stir up anger against Israel to divert the pressure of popular opinion. If Syria's economy continues to stagnate (and that may be its best hope given that violence there is disrupting trade and scaring off investors), Assad may try to seize on anti-Israeli sentiment to deflect popular anger and adopt more confrontational policies.

Israel's fear of Iran is growing as a result of this uncertainty. U.S. and Israeli officials accuse Iran, and its ally Hezbollah, of helping the Syrian regime crush peaceful demonstrators.[17] Iran worries that unrest could spread to its soil, but it also comforts itself by claiming that unrest in the Arab world is proof that the people there reject Westernized regimes, like Mubarak's and Tunisia's Zine El Abidine Ben Ali, and want more religion in their lives.[18] This may not jibe with the reality of the revolutions so far, but Iran nevertheless is riding high and may be more aggressive in backing Hezbollah, Hamas, or other allies in the region.

As most of the above concerns suggest, Israel is a status quo power in many ways. While Israelis bemoan their situation, the country's position is strong. Terrorism is down from the high levels of ten years ago. Israel is the military giant in the region. Its economy is strong and growing stronger. So change, even if it means the toppling of regional foes, risks rocking this prosperous boat.

> Israel is a status quo power in many ways.

Down with the People

In the past, Israel used the lack of democracy in the Arab world to justify its special closeness to the United States and its isolation in the region. Israel was an island of democracy in a sea of dictatorship, and as such had a special affinity for the United States, the world's oldest and most powerful democracy. Netanyahu used to argue that democracy was vital for true peace, as undemocratic countries were not trustworthy and thus might not honor any treaty they signed. He tempered these views after Hamas won elections in Gaza in 2006, and now seems to have shelved them completely.[19] Democracy, it seems, is not necessarily welcome.

Given how strong anti-Israel sentiment is in much of the Arab world, Israelis do not trust public opinion. A 2010 University of Maryland/Zogby poll found that almost 90 percent of Arabs saw Israel as "the biggest threat to you."[20] "The ugly facts," said former Defense Minister Moshe Arens, "are that the two peace treaties that Israel concluded so far—the one with Egypt and the other with Jordan—were both signed with dictators: Anwar Sadat and King Hussein."[21] In other words, Israelis fear that the Mubaraks, Husseins, and other dictators are as good as it will get for Israel *because* these leaders are outside the mainstream of their societies.

Crisis Points

Most of the above concerns are ineffable and long-term, though their vagueness makes them no less potent. While Israel may plan for these problems, many will not pan out. More immediately, the dramatic changes in the Arab world are likely to exacerbate two important security issues for Israel: its confrontation with the Hamas government of the Gaza Strip and the status of the peace process.

The Coming Crisis in Gaza

Since Hamas took control of Gaza in 2007, Israel has tried to contain and undermine the Islamist regime with a mix of diplomatic isolation, economic pressure, and occasional military strikes. To intimidate Hamas, Israel also retains the threat of a more massive military response, such as the 2008–2009 "Cast Lead" operation, which led to more than 1,000 Palestinian deaths. Despite this considerable pressure, Hamas has consolidated power and is steadily building up its armed forces. It now has rockets that can reach well beyond Israeli towns near Gaza such as Sderot and can hit major cities like Ashkelon, Ashdod, Beersheba, and perhaps even Tel Aviv.

At the same time, since Cast Lead, Hamas largely has adhered to a ceasefire, at times allowing groups like Palestine Islamic Jihad or salafi–jihadist organizations with an ideology more akin to Osama bin Laden's to strike Israel, but not using its own forces. Hamas is now the government of Gaza, and as such it focuses not only on fighting Israel, but also on the prosperity of Gaza (or, more accurately, preventing Gaza's disastrous economic situation from getting worse) and shoring up its political position there.

Under Mubarak, Egypt quietly helped Israel against Hamas, much to Hamas' outrage. Egypt mostly kept the Rafah crossing point between Egypt and Gaza closed, helping Israel restrict the flow of goods and people into and out of Gaza. Over time, a massive tunnel complex between Egypt and Gaza developed, and Israeli officials complained that a mix of incompetence, corruption, and sympathy kept Egypt from shutting these down. Israelis, however, recognized that Egypt could be far more helpful to Hamas, and thus muted their criticism even as they pressed Cairo to be more aggressive. And in the last months of Mubarak's rule, Egypt heeded Israel's call, building a barrier on the border that extended deep underground, making tunneling much harder.

The revolution in Egypt and unrest elsewhere in the Arab world has shaken this always-fragile equilibrium. Sympathy for Gazans in Egypt is high, and Hamas' resistance to Israel is also popular. Rami Khoury observes that there is "widespread indignity felt by Egyptians who see themselves as the jailers of Gaza on behalf of Israel and Washington."[22] Any Egyptian regime that reflects popular opinion will (the interim government announced in May that it plans to open Rafah soon) release pressure on Gaza by easing restrictions on the Rafah crossing point and looking the other way at smuggling. This would probably be the least that a popularly elected regime could get away with, and there would be pressure to directly aid Gaza and Hamas, not just end restrictions. Already the new Egyptian government announced it will open Rafah and no longer cooperate with the economic isolation of Gaza. Egyptian Foreign Minister Nabil El-Arabi declared "Egyptian national security and Palestinian security are one."[23]

Should pressure ease, and should Hamas—as is likely—exploit this to acquire weapons and send personnel in and out for training, Israel will be tempted to take unilateral action. This may involve operations on or near the Egyptian side of the border of Gaza, as well as increasing the pace of killing Hamas leaders in Gaza. Such actions, in turn, would inflame popular sentiment in Egypt further against Israel and increase pressure on any regime in Cairo to further aid Hamas.

Hamas too may be bolder. Where Israel sees a loss of an ally in Egypt, Hamas sees a potential friend, particularly if the Muslim Brotherhood enjoys increased influence in Egypt. Hamas can now play to the Egyptian people even if the Egyptian military and any elected leaders prefer to avoid a confrontation with Israel.

Even more important, popular opinion will play an increasing role in Gaza. Hamas is not immune from the demands for change sweeping the region. The ceasefire Hamas largely has observed has damaged its credentials, increasing its incentives to fight Israel as a resistance organization, and now it needs those credentials. On March 18, Hamas fired more than 30 mortars at Israel and claimed responsibility, justifying the attack as revenge for an Israeli airstrike that killed two Hamas members. On April 7, an anti-tank weapon fired from Gaza hit an Israeli school bus, mortally wounding a 16 year-old boy and the bus driver. Israel responded with military strikes on Gaza

> Hamas may look to get its credentials as a resistance organization back.

that killed three militants and three civilians. The unity agreement with Abbas also shows the increased importance Hamas now attaches to placating public opinion.

Hamas may seek to burnish its resistance credentials in order to counter any legitimacy loss from its authoritarian ways. On a rhetorical level, this may involve measures such as Hamas leader and Gaza Prime Minister Ismail Haniyeh's praising of Osama bin Laden after the United States killed him on May 1—the only leader of a (pseudo) state to do so. Hamas will also find it harder to back down from its on-again, off-again confrontations with Israel. Even if Hamas itself does not engage in attacks, more radical groups like Palestine Islamic Jihad and salafi–jihadists will still attack Israel, and Hamas may fear that cracking down on them would hurt it politically.

Poor Prospects for Peace

Beyond the usual reasons that peace is desirable—security for Israel, justice and dignity for the Palestinians, and greater stability for the region—a successful peace process would take away one of the greatest rhetorical weapons of extremists and make it harder for demagogues to create an escalatory spiral. It would also improve Israel's relations with the United States and Europe at a key moment in the region's history. Israel, however, will be even more skeptical of taking risks for peace. For now, the long-term identity of Netanyahu's peace partner is an open question. If Mubarak can go, so too can Abbas or Assad. So why, Israelis ask, take risks for peace if your partner may be gone tomorrow?

Nor are Arab leaders likely to extend a hand. New leaders of nascent democracies are not likely to risk their popularity by embracing a peace which, under most conceivable scenarios, would be seen by their own people as selling out the Palestinians. Battered old regimes are also less likely to embrace a peace which would not be popular with their constituents when their own legitimacy is suspect. Palestinian leaders will be less compromising. Abbas, for example, is already under pressure because of his authoritarian ways in the West Bank, and the charge of "sellout" might topple his regime.

Should actual negotiations commence, Israeli demands for security guarantees are likely to grow. One Israeli analyst called for demands to include "a demilitarized Palestine, Israel's right to respond to terror attacks, and an Israeli military presence along the Jordan River."[24] Some of these demands have been accepted in a de facto way by Palestinian negotiators (like a demilitarized Palestinian state), but others represent a more hardline stance than previous Israeli positions.

Given Israel's overwhelming conventional military superiority, and the unlikely prospect that impoverished Syria or a new, revolutionary regime in Jordan could suddenly field a strong conventional military, these demands are not strategic but political, meant to reassure the Israeli public in an uncertain time. But they are political on the Palestinian side too, and acceptance of additional Israeli security demands would tell many Palestinians that their sovereignty means little in practice—so little, in fact, that Israeli troops could stay along their borders and go into their cities without interference.

America Caught in Between

The United States will be caught between its commitment to Israel and its desire to gain the goodwill of the new Arab leaders and advance democratization in the region. U.S. regional interests go well beyond the security of Israel, of course, embracing issues from counterterrorism to energy security.

The peace process is an obvious point of potential contention. One way to make the success of the Arab Spring more likely is to remove one of the greatest radicalizing forces in the region—the Palestinian question—from the agenda. New governments and old will want the United States to once again beat its head against the wall in hopes of a breakthrough. For Israelis, peace was not about being welcomed in the Arab world. Aluf Benn argues that "most Israelis viewed the peace process as a means for bettering relations with Europe and the United States and not as a channel to regional acceptance."[25] Well before the Arab Spring began, the Obama and Netanyahu administrations had locked horns on this issue.

The divisions within the Palestinian camp, the rightward shift in Israeli politics, and the coming election in the United States already made this peace-process season unlikely to bear fruit, but the Arab revolutions mean it will be almost impossible. The result will be the triumph of form over substance. Miller contends that "in the coming months we'll see a lot of process but not much peace."[26] Even an empty process, however, can lead to disputes, particularly if the Obama administration believes Netanyahu and company are refusing to put a serious proposal on the table.

Gaza offers the risk of a high-profile crisis that both the new leaders and the United States would rather avoid. The United States, however, will find it hard to press Israel to restrain itself in Gaza if Hamas becomes more aggressive. Mortar attacks and shootings from Gaza deserve an Israeli response, but a new regime in Egypt, unlike Mubarak, may not play ball with Israel.

Israel's fears are much more likely to become reality if reform efforts stall or fail. Like it or not, Mubarak is gone. The *ancien regime* will not return in Cairo, and pro-Western allies from Bahrain to Morocco are shaken. It's worth thinking about what the failure of democracy in Egypt would look like. Failure would empower radicals in Egypt and throughout the region, "proving" that a Western, democratic model is not right for the Arab world. Reformers would point to a lack of Western support, while critics would use U.S. support for Israel as a cudgel to beat back moderates. More extreme voices would only gain resonance.

Should regimes start to fail, scapegoating becomes more likely. Anti-Israel sentiment has long been a way for dictatorships to deflect popular dissatisfaction with the regime, and new rulers will use this tool too. If these regimes suffer economic and political problems, the political logic of scapegoating grows.

Conversely, if regime legitimacy grows because new leaders enjoy the consent of the governed and are showing material progress on political and economic grounds, the need for scapegoating diminishes. Israeli President Shimon Peres has contended that "poverty and oppression in the region have fed resentment against Israel and the better our neighbors will have it, we shall have better neighbors."[27]

Scapegoating, however, may avail new regimes little if they cannot govern well. Indeed, one positive sign for Israel regarding the Arab Spring is that it is not about Israel. The Syrian uprising in particular shows that Arab publics will not buy regime attempts to deflect their anger over corruption, stagnation, and repression at home onto Israel. Scapegoating is more likely to succeed, however, if Israel's policies are viewed as provocative and uncompromising.

The success of democratization in Egypt is particularly important. Egypt's size will always make it important, but its political stature in the region fell under Mubarak's sclerotic rule. Now, as the likely leader of the Arab democratic camp, it will again enjoy enormous prestige. Indeed, Israeli fears that Iran will exploit the void can best be countered by a politically strong Egypt that enjoys credibility with the Arab people and offers a more powerful message than what Tehran promotes.

Under these new circumstances, Egypt's peace treaty with Israel could become particularly important. No longer is it a deal of elites. Now, the Egyptian nation will be embracing it in a de facto way, making it easier for leaders in other countries to convince their own people that an unpopular peace may be the best they can hope for given today's political and strategic realities.

In the end, regional revolutions can work to Israel's benefit. Change, however, must be managed properly. Israel in particular must recognize the new regional dynamics, including the potential for escalation and the political realities of its neighbors and potential peace partners. Such recognition will not make the new challenges go away, but they will make Israel ready to seize opportunities for peace and less likely to engage in a dangerous escalation that could spiral into disaster.

> In the end, regional revolutions can work to Israel's benefit.

Notes

1. Janine Zacharia, "Israel wary of transition in Egypt, concerned about regional stability," *The Washington Post*, February 2, 2011, http://www.washingtonpost.com/national/israel-worries-about-peace-amid-regional-tumult/2011/02/01/ABZtFbE_story.html.

2. Rebecca Anna Stoil, "EU officials meet in Knesset, but eyes are on Egypt," *Jerusalem Post*, February 8, 2011, http://www.jpost.com/DiplomacyAndPolitics/Article.aspx?ID=207272&R=R1.

3. Benjamin Netanyahu, "PM Netanyahu addresses the Knesset: The situation in Egypt," February 2, 2011, http://www.mfa.gov.il/MFA/Government/Speeches+by+Israeli+leaders/2011/PM_Netanyahu_addresses_Knesset_situation_Egypt_2-Feb-2011.htm.

4. Aluf Benn, "Overcoming Fear and Anxiety in Tel Aviv," *Foreign Affairs*, February 8, 2011, http://www.foreignaffairs.com/articles/67353/aluf-benn/overcoming-fear-and-anxiety-in-tel-aviv.

5. Eli Lake, "Muslim Brotherhood seeks end to Israel treaty," *Washington Times*, February 3, 2011, http://www.washingtontimes.com/news/2011/feb/3/muslim-brotherhood-seeks-end-to-israel-treaty/.

6. Yossi Klein Halevi, "Israel's Neighborhood Watch," *Foreign Affairs*, February 1, 2011, http://www.foreignaffairs.com/articles/67344/yossi-klein-halevi/israels-neighborhood-watch.

7. Barry Rubin, "Arab World: The bad news from Egypt," *Jerusalem Post*, February 18, 2011, http://www.jpost.com/Features/FrontLines/Article.aspx?id=208741.

8. Zacharia, "Israel wary of transition in Egypt, concerned about regional stability."

9. Jason Burke, "Amr Moussa, Secretary General of the Arab League," *The Guardian*, March 21, 2011, http://www.guardian.co.uk/world/2011/mar/21/amr-moussa-secretary-general-arab-league.

10. Steven Erlanger, "Upheaval Jolts Israel and Raises New Worry," *New York Times*, February 23, 2011, http://www.nytimes.com/2011/02/24/world/middleeast/24arabs.html.

11. Aaron David Miller, "Why Israel Fears a Free Egypt," *Washington Post*, February 4, 2011, http://www.washingtonpost.com/opinions/why-israel-fears-a-free-egypt/2011/02/04/ABu9pxQ_story.html.

12. Pew Global Attitudes Project, "Egyptians Embrace Revolt Leaders, Religious Parties and Military, As Well," April 25, 2011, http://pewglobal.org/files/2011/04/Pew-Global-Attitudes-Egypt-Report-FINAL-April-25-2011.pdf."

13. Moshe Arens, "Growing Mideast Democracy Could Benefit Israel Too," *Haaretz.com*, April 5, 2011, http://www.haaretz.com/print-edition/opinion/growing-mideast-democracy-could-benefit-israel-too-1.354143.

14. Erlanger, "Upheaval Jolts Israel and Raises New Worry."

15. Benn, "Overcoming Fear and Anxiety in Tel Aviv."

16. Khaled Abu Toameh, "Will the Palestinians Rise Up Too?" *Jerusalem Post*, March 11, 2011, http://www.jpost.com/Features/FrontLines/Article.aspx?id=211680.

17. Adam Entous and Matthew Rosenberg, "U.S. Says Iran Helps Crackdown in Syria," *Wall Street Journal*, April 14, 2011, http://online.wsj.com/article/SB10001424052748704547804576261222747330438.html?mod=WSJ_topics_obama; "Israel Believes Iran and Hezbollah Aiding Syria Crackdown," *Haaretz News Service*, March 27, 2011, http://www.haaretz.com/news/international/israel-believes-iran-and-hezbollah-aiding-syria-crackdown-1.352086.

18. Mehrun Etebari, "How Tehran Sees Tunis," ForeignPolicy.com, January 28, 2011, http://www.foreignpolicy.com/articles/2011/01/28/how_tehran_sees_tunis.

19. Benn, "Overcoming Fear and Anxiety in Tel Aviv."

20. University of Maryland and Zogby International, "2010 Arab Public Opinion Poll," August 5, 2010, http://www.brookings.edu/~/media/Files/rc/reports/2010/08_arab_opinion_poll_telhami/08_arab_opinion_poll_telhami.pdf.

21. Isabel Kershner, "Egypt's Upheaval Hardens Israel's Stance on Peace," *New York Times*, February 2, 2011, http://www.nytimes.com/2011/02/03/world/middleeast/03israel.html?scp=56&sq=Isabel+Kershner&st=nyt.

22. Erlanger, "Upheaval Jolts Israel and Raises New Worry."

23. Elior Levy, "Egypt to Open Rafah Crossing," Ynetnews.com, April 29, 2011, http://www.ynetnews.com/articles/0,7340,L-4062118,00.html.

24. Halevi, "Israel's Neighborhood Watch."

25. Benn, "Overcoming Fear and Anxiety in Tel Aviv."

26. Aaron David Miller, "2011: The Year of the (Bad) Initiative," *New York Times*, March 11, 2011, http://www.nytimes.com/2011/03/12/opinion/12iht-edmiller12.html.

27. "Mideast Revolutions Could Be Good for Israel, Says Peres," *Haaretz.com*, March 28, 2011, http://www.haaretz.com/news/diplomacy-defense/mideast-revolutions-could-be-good-for-israel-says-peres-1.352374.

Bruce W. Jentleson

Beware the Duck Test

In explaining why the United States was scheming to overthrow the government of Guatemala—democratically elected but allegedly with communist leanings during the Cold War—the U.S. ambassador proposed the "duck test": "Many times it is impossible to prove legally that a certain individual is a communist; but for cases of this sort I recommend a practical method of detection—the 'duck test'....[If a] bird certainly looks like a duck. Also, he goes to the pond and you notice he swims like a duck. Well, by this time you've probably reached the conclusion that the bird is a duck, whether he's wearing a label or not."[1]

The duck test lumping together leaders, parties, and movements which in any way smacked of radicalism as part of the Soviet orbit was a key factor in many U.S. foreign policy failures during the Cold War in the then-Third World. As we focus on an Arab world undergoing unprecedented change and instability, posing threats but also presenting opportunities, we need to avoid making comparable mistakes with respect to political Islam and other forces. Blithe generalizations, binary thinking, and fear-mongering distort both the political dialogue and the analytic capacity needed to pursue policies differentiated according to the particular political dynamics of the various countries of the Arab world and the strategic challenges facing the United States.

Lessons Learned

There is no question that the Soviets were a threat in the Third World. They helped start the Korean War. They invaded Afghanistan. They took advantage

Bruce W. Jentleson is a Professor at Duke University, Sanford School of Public Policy. From 2009–2011, he served as Senior Advisor to the State Department Policy Planning Director. He is also an Editorial Board Member for TWQ. His most recent book is The End of Arrogance: America in the Global Competition of Ideas, with Steven Weber (Harvard University Press, 2010). He would like to thank Hal Brands for his helpful comments and numerous others for insightful discussions. He can be reached at bwj7@duke.edu.

Copyright © 2011 Center for Strategic and International Studies
The Washington Quarterly • 34:3 pp. 137–149
DOI: 10.1080/0163660X.2011.588169

of Fidel Castro's fervent anti-Americanism. They supported subversion and sought out beachheads in various places at various times of the Cold War. But in many instances, the monolithic view of global communism and concomitant failure to make national differentiations inherent in the duck test and its three corollaries—"Anybody But a Communist," "Our SOB," and the Munich "appeasement" analogy—both undermined American ideals and damaged American strategic interests.

Just as the duck test determined whom we opposed, we supported "ABC": Anybody But a Communist. Unsavory alliances with dictators, support for military coups, covert actions, and other policies which hardly fit with democracy promotion were justified with the overriding strategic rationale that "he may be an SOB, but he's our SOB." Anything other than staunch support for those ABCs–SOBs was derided—indeed, delegitimized—as akin to British Prime Minister Neville Chamberlain's attempted appeasement of Adolf Hitler at Munich in 1938.[2]

Much of the failure of U.S. Vietnam policy traces back to these four strategic miscalculations. Hans Morgenthau, the iconic realist, opposed the Vietnam War as early as 1967, arguing in anti-duck test terms that even without converting Ho Chi Minh from communism, a relationship could be developed that would "prevent such a communist revolution from turning against the United States."[3] Instead, Ngo Dinh Diem was hailed as the Winston Churchill of Asia, that is until the United States colluded in his assassination and embraced one ABC–SOB after another while one president after another invoked the Munich analogy. "We learned from Hitler at Munich," President Lyndon B. Johnson stated in 1965 as a key part of the explanation for the initial major increase in U.S. troops, "that success only feeds the appetite of aggression. The battle would be renewed...bringing with it perhaps even larger and crueler conflict, as we learned from the lessons of history." Seven years later, President Richard Nixon made his case for escalating the war, including mining North Vietnamese harbors, in the Munich-like terms that "an American defeat in Viet-Nam would encourage this kind of aggression all over the world."[4]

A similar pattern pervaded Latin America. President John F. Kennedy proclaimed his oft-cited statement that "those who make peaceful change impossible make violent revolution inevitable" on the first anniversary of the Alliance for Progress, itself hailed by JFK on its founding as "an alliance of free governments [that] must work to eliminate tyranny from a hemisphere in which it has no rightful place."[5] But when put to the test, as Latin American elites and militaries resisted peaceful change and resorted to coups to protect their own interests, the United States fell back on duck tests and ABC definitions. In the 1964 Brazil coup, for example, U.S. "enthusiasm" for the coup "was so palpable that Washington sent its congratulations even before the new regime could be installed."[6] Among the torture victims at the hands of the military regime over its two decades in power was Dilma Rousseff, the current president of Brazil.

And in Iran, "our SOB" support for the Shah ended up as lose–lose for both U.S. ideals and interests. In Washington, it "inhibited intelligence collection, dampened policymakers' appetite for analysis of the Shah's position, and deafened policymakers to the warning implicit in the available current intelligence."[7] The Carter administration did put some pressure on the Shah to liberalize, but so little that as late as November 1978, policy options other than support for the Shah were "inadmissible." Even as the crisis heightened, Carter still "directed that we get the Shah's approval before talking to moderate opposition leaders." Carter wouldn't go so far as to support a military coup or other "iron fist" responses, but he also didn't get out from under "the catastrophic illusion that, because we support a foreign country, our vital interests are in every way congruent with the interest of that country as perceived by the government in power."[8] Instead, U.S. policy stuck to the Munich-like rationale that "other rulers in the region, friendly to the United States, were watching us closely. How we responded to the crisis was a guide to them for how we might react if they were threatened."[9]

As we strategize for the challenges posed by the Arab Spring, the past need not be prologue. While learning the right lessons from the Cold War won't assure success, not learning them makes failure more likely.

The Arab World Today

Let's start with the one certainty about where the Arab world is going: we don't know. Nobody knows. Where the *ancien regimes* have fallen, as in Tunisia and Egypt, the unifying effect of a shared objective has given way to mixes of electoral contestation, behind-the-scenes maneuvering, waves of repression against some of those who led the

There is one certainty about where the Arab world is going: we don't know.

revolutions, and outbreaks of sectarian violence such as between Muslims and Coptic Christians in Egypt. Where old regimes are struggling to hang on, it's not clear whether they can and what it will take to do so, or if they can't what would come next. Even best-case scenarios must bear in mind that democracy does not spring forth like Athena from Zeus' head. At best it takes years, even decades, to institutionalize. "It's an entire country that needs to be remade," a Tunisian mayor observed. "It's not going to be one year, or two years, or three years. It's going to be an entire generation."[10]

Nor is this just about politics. Sufficient progress must be made on the pervasive economic problems and social injustices which feed the unrest. Sources of instability and building blocks for prosperity go back to the "triple deficits"—education, women's empowerment, and political freedom— highlighted in the 2002 *Arab Human Development Report*.[11] Closing or at least narrowing these deficits requires not just higher GDP growth rates and foreign investment flows, but also greater equity and benefits extending beyond elites into broader societies. Yet the gap between the rich and poor had been widening in recent years, and made all the more grating as with the spate of gated communities built in and around Cairo. "The ominous dynamics of marginalization" was the warning sounded in the 2009 *Arab Human Development Report*.[12] All too exemplary was the Yemeni village left so destitute that it turned to al-Qaeda in the Arabian Peninsula (AQAP) to provide teachers for its schools.

The Arab–Israeli conflict, in particular the Israeli–Palestinian dimension, also continues to be a factor—not as much as some claim, but not as little as others do.

> **F**our lessons from the past can help navigate the uncertainties ahead.

With many in Israel now even warier of peace agreements and Arab regimes potentially resorting even more frequently to the diversionary script of invoking the Zionist enemy, progress on peace may now be that much harder. Yet it is that much more essential. Then there is Iran, discussed below, and post-bin Laden al-Qaeda. Navigating these and other uncertainties is an enormous challenge. Four lessons from the past can help.

No Duck Test for Political Islam

Political Islam is neither inherently incompatible with democracy nor automatically antagonistic toward the United States. There are "many faces of political Islam," as the scholar Mohammed Ayoob put it even before the Arab Spring.[13] While transnational links to al-Qaeda, Iran, or such others need to be taken into account, they must not automatically subsume national differentiations. Within those national differentiations, further assessments must be made of the goals, strategies, visions, and leadership of the respective parties and movements. Policies need to be tailored to oppose those inimical to our values and threatening our interests, while remaining open to those with which coexistence and cooperation may be possible, even though we have differences.

In Egypt, for example, this means getting beyond the essentialist view of the Muslim Brotherhood as a singular organic entity driven by an absolutist ideology unchanging over time. This is "a caricature that exaggerates certain features of the Brotherhood while ignoring others, and underestimates the extent to which the group has changed over time."[14] Islamist dispositions do persist, but there are divisions within the current leadership. These cut a number of ways based on relative emphases on political engagement and social work, conservative versus progressive interpretations of Islam, and generational factors. How these play out is not endogenous to the Brotherhood, but also affected by the broader political dynamics of the new Egyptian system in which it must compete. The amount of political space available depends in part on how appealing other political parties or leaders are and how strong the political institutions are to sustain the rules of the game and keep the Brotherhood to its approach of "participation not domination."[15]

> The Muslim Brotherhood is not a singular organic entity.

Even many of those within the U.S. foreign policy debate most concerned about the Muslim Brotherhood stress engaging it rather than seeking to isolate it. Engagement includes applying pressure, setting conditions, and articulating redlines. But it is quite different than duck-test antagonism. It recognizes that U.S. policy is not just affected *by* the Brotherhood, but also affects *it*. In social science parlance, U.S. policy is not just the dependent variable responding, but also an independent variable affecting what the Muslim Brotherhood is and does. This cautions against assuming that the Brotherhood "would automatically become pragmatic should it take power," [16] as Daniel Byman prudently advises. It also checks against just erring on the side of supposed caution with a hedging strategy which risks making the worst case more rather than less likely. Among the ways to strike this balance are focusing on whether elections are free and fair, not on who wins, and adherence to the commitment to peace with Israel consistent with the Camp David Treaty while at least tacitly accepting that, as we already have started to see, a new Egyptian regime will take a different overall approach to the peace process.

Comparable differentiations hold for other Arab countries. In most countries where the Muslim Brotherhood operates, "it seeks only peaceful political change; it rejects violence as a way of securing its goals; and the rejection of violence is not a mere tactical adjustment but a deep strategic commitment."[17] In Tunisia, while secular Tunisians express some anxiety about the political strength the Ennahda movement is showing, they also acknowledge that "political parties influenced by Islam are inevitable in their prospective democracy." With that as a baseline, the worry is about more extremist Islamic groups, but the calculation is that those groups are more likely to *gain* traction if the system is perceived as inimical to any and all political Islam.[18]

In Bahrain, Shiite groups such as al-Haq and al-Wafa do appear to have links to and be receiving assistance from Iran. In Yemen, while AQAP has not been driving the unrest, it is opportunistically seeking to exploit it. In Libya, the activities of al-Qaeda in the Islamic Maghreb (AQIM) and other extremists have gone from what the top NATO commander initially called "flickers" to what an Algerian official termed an "increasingly noticeable presence."[19] Yet, there are other and larger Shiite groups in Bahrain such as the al-Wefaq movement that do not have Iranian links and have much more of a Bahraini–Arab identity and agenda; in Yemen, the array of groups aligned against President Ali Abdullah Saleh is very diverse, including former top government and military officials whose democratic credentials are not exactly pristine but are hardly jihadist; and in Libya, the National Transitional Council is largely secular and includes political Islamists not linked to AQIM or other extremists.

> The United States cannot credibly push for political change if it excludes all political Islam.

In sum, political Islam is likely to be a part of the political mix more often than not. Some versions are ducks, some are not. They have to be differentiated. The United States cannot credibly push for political change if it excludes all political Islam.

Don't Go from "ABC" to "ABT"

U.S. national security will continue to require counterterrorism cooperation from Arab governments. But we have to stop substituting "ABT" (Anybody But Terrorists) for the Cold War Anybody but Communists. That approach has, in part, trapped the United States in the regional box it is now trying to escape— trying to avoid supporting unpopular, corrupt regimes whose principal claim to leadership is that terrorists will take over if they do not rule. For years, we looked the other way regarding Hosni Mubarak's increasingly autocratic rule in exchange for his cooperation on counterterrorism. No wonder he tried to play the terrorist threat card during the Tahrir Square demonstrations. With President Saleh in Yemen, we've had even more active collaboration, including permission to conduct drone attacks and other operations inside Yemen in exchange for substantial U.S. support in his battles with the Houthis and various other rivals. Even Muammar Qaddafi had been providing some enemy-of-my-enemy-is-my-friend cooperation against AQIM. And to go a bit afield to Pakistan, for all the aid and blind eye we've provided under the ABT rationale, even before the capture and killing of Osama bin Laden, the Obama administration could only say it was "vexing" why the Pakistani government and military continued to lack the will for "defeating the insurgency in Pakistan."[20]

The point is not democracy purism. We may hope for a world in which our relationships are "OWD" (Only With Democracies), but we have to live in and strategize for a world when that is sometimes not an option. But for all the realpolitik claims the ABC policy pushed during the Cold War and the ABT policy has made post-9/11, such a rationale reverses the leverage in relationships, giving it to leaders who think the United States can be spooked into giving them blank checks. Mubarak could continue to be all the more autocratic, corrupt, and able to rebuff U.S. "suggestions" for reform by invoking the terrorist threat. When Saleh needed Yemeni troops and intelligence operations to try to keep himself in power, he diverted them from counterterrorism locales and missions. Even before the current crisis, there were indications that he was keeping AQAP alive just enough to buttress his leverage over us, yet not too much to lose his claim to counterterrorism cooperation.[21] In Libya, Qaddafi's propagandizing the rebellion as AQIM-led is belied by little such evidence, including the statement by the Libyan Interim Transitional National Council pledging "commitment to the implementation of the relevant Security Council resolutions on Counter-Terrorism, including the resolutions on the sanctions concerning al-Qaeda and Taliban."[22]

No question there are terrorism risks amidst instability as well as regarding the shape successor regimes take. But what we've been seeing these past months is the risks of ABT strategies. And now potential opportunities are being opened up for alternative paths toward societal changes that help to counter jihadism more organically than any U.S. policy mix of counterterrorism and public diplomacy can. It's telling that Ayman al-Zawahiri, al-Qaeda's long-time number two, railed against the Arab Spring as misguided since "justice, freedom and independence" can only be achieved through "jihad and resistance until the Islamic regime rises."[23] A higher bar for U.S. support than just ABT thus has a strategic basis, not just a normative one; it's about interests not just ideals.

"Our SOB" OBE

The "our SOB" option has not only shown flaws over the years, changes in the 21st-century world have left it OBE (Overtaken By Events). For one thing, states are now less convinced that being "ours" is in their own security interests, unlike during the Cold War. While they still want U.S. security assistance and protection to the extent that it serves their needs and interests, they also want to be free to pursue their own policies and initiatives not subject to Washington's approval, and the United States no longer has the leverage of the Soviet threat to play against them.

The Saudis, for example, have made that very clear amidst the Arab Spring. King Abdullah was widely reported to have expressed his indignation, and more, in a call to President Obama during the Egyptian crisis. They intervened along with the United Arab Emirates in fellow Gulf Cooperation Council member Bahrain in March 2011 over the objection of the United States in the name of GCC "common responsibility" and "common destiny." King Abdullah then rebuffed a visit from Secretary of State Hillary Clinton and Secretary of Defense Robert Gates. When a few weeks later Secretary Gates was received, Bahrain was said to be off limits for discussion. Although Iran has remained on the U.S.–Saudi shared agenda, the differences over Bahrain indicate differences over how best to counter Iranian influence.

While fueled by some factors particular to the Middle East, this strategic shift actually is part of a broader global trend toward what Steve Weber and I elsewhere call a transition from a Ptolemaic world to a Copernican one. [24] Just as Ptolemy held the Earth to be at the center with all the other planets, indeed the whole solar system, revolving around it, so was the United States seen as at the center of the Cold War world—the wielder of power, the economic engine, the bastion of free-world ideology. When the Cold War ended with the United States as the sole surviving superpower, the U.S. economy driving globalization, and democracy sweeping the planet, the world seemed even more Ptolemaic.

But broad global forces such as the diffusion of power, pluralization of diplomacy, eastward and southward shifts in economic dynamism, and the intensification of national identities have been making this 21st-century world much more of a Copernican one. The Earth (a.k.a. the United States) is not at the center. Other planets/states have their own orbits in which they define their foreign policies more in terms of their own national interests and less in pro- or anti-U.S. terms of reference. Thus, the Indian national security adviser stressed on the eve of President Obama's November 2010 visit that although India seeks better relations with the United States, its foreign policy remains one of "genuine non-alignment." [25] The debate about whether Turkey has become anti-Western and pro-Islamism misses the ways in which nationalist logic has become important, as expressed by a Turkish foreign ministry official: "We have [historically] waited for the big powers to make up their minds on big issues and we just follow them. For the past several years, we have made up our own minds." [26] With Brazil, while some anti-Americanism is sprinkled in, the drive is much more about its own national narrative of greatness going back to its founding. [27] While the United States still has some gravitational pull/leverage over others, it tends to be well short of making a country "ours" even in policy terms, whether in the Middle East or elsewhere.

Another aspect of being OBE is how much harder it now is for regimes to sustain SOB-ness at home. What started in Tunisia and spread to Egypt, Libya, Syria, Bahrain, Yemen, and beyond is what might be called the "Wizard of Oz" effect. Recall the scene when Dorothy pulls back the curtain and reveals that the great and powerful Oz was nothing more than a small unimposing man. The fall of the first Arab dictator punctured the aura of leader invincibility and countered the sense of popular powerlessness, and did so with a transnational demonstration effect. "Generations believed we could do nothing," one protester affirmed, "and now, in a matter of weeks, we know that we can."[28] This sense of empowerment is coming to the "youth bulge" generation—about 60 percent of the population in the Arab world is under 30, the median age around 26—who already didn't buy as much into the heroic narrative of anti-colonialism which palliated the demands of their parents and grandparents.

While too much sometimes gets made of this as the "Facebook–Twitter" revolution, technology clearly was a major driver of this empowerment. Information and communication always are key to reform and revolution. During the Cold War, Soviet dissidents like Andrei Sakharov, Alexsandr Solzhenitsyn, and Soviet Jews improvised their *samizdat*, reproducing documents with carbon paper, Xeroxing, or whatever other methods were available. Facebook–Twitter are samizdat on steroids, so much faster and with such wider reach. This has been especially influential for young women in traditional villages, allowing them "to bypass the men—fathers, brothers, husbands—who circumscribed their worlds and their ability to communicate. They cannot go to the park unaccompanied and meet friends, but they can join a chat room or send instant messages."[29]

It is important to stress that it is harder for governments to go the repressive route, but not impossible. The Assad dictatorship's heavy hand may quiet things down. The GCC intervention in Bahrain may buttress their fellow monarchy. Economic concessions such as the $128 billion package the Saudi regime suddenly bestowed on its people, and political tactics such as the Bahraini palace launching its own "We are all Hamad" (the King) Facebook page and the Foreign Minister tweeting "Yes we can!" may assuage the public.[30] But they may not. Neither scenario should be dismissed from U.S. strategizing, nor should they be assumed. Those curtains that have been pulled can never be fully closed again, the technologies not closed out.

Flaws in the Munich/Iran Analogy

The 1979 Iran analogy is today's Munich equivalent. Sometimes it is explicitly articulated. Other times it's implicit in questions like "do we know who the opposition is" and leery "what if..." formulations. Islamism was the main driver of the Iranian revolution: it has not been the main driver of any of the Arab Spring revolutions and opposition movements thus far. If Egypt, Tunisia, Bahrain, or any other country were to go extremist Islamist, it would be more through its own dynamics than ones analogous to Iran. There also are democratic examples from Turkey and Indonesia of indigenous political Islamist parties coming to power. This is not to say that these necessarily apply any better to current cases, only that they demonstrate that no single analogy inherently pertains.

> The 1979 Iran analogy is today's Munich equivalent.

Furthermore, today we have not seen the anti-Americanism that so fueled the Iranian revolution. This was particularly striking in Egypt, where the U.S. relationship with Mubarak was akin to that with the Shah. Yet, even with some of the Obama administration's equivocations, Tahrir Square stayed anti-regime but not anti-American. A recent poll showed 58 percent of Egyptians favoring close or closer relations with the United States.[31] The Bahraini protesters have not been demanding removal of the U.S. Fifth Fleet base. These dynamics may change. If they do, though, it will be because of policies pursued and events that transpire over time, not Iran-like roots in the revolution.

Roots or no roots, a variation of Iran as Munich warns of Iranian opportunistic meddling in the instability, and urges taking a stand against any such possibility. This was the rationale for the GCC intervention in Bahrain against "an external threat on the whole Gulf." In mid-April, with the Saudis in the lead, the GCC protested to the UN Security Council "flagrant Iranian interference and provocations." They even used the language "take the necessary measures," stopping just short of "all," which had been the phrasing in Security Council resolutions authorizing the use of force against Libya the month before and against Iraq back in 1990 following the invasion of Kuwait.[32]

While there is an Iranian element that has to be strategized against, making it the dominant element would be yet another past-as-prologue path to policy failure. In trying to strike a balance, the Obama administration not only has to navigate Gulf diplomacy, it also has to protect its right flank in politics at home. That Obama got Osama clearly helps. But with Iran still such a hot button issue politically, any inkling that Iran may be making gains—actual, potential, or even grossly exaggerated—will feed Munich analogizing, especially in an election year.

Broader Regional Restrategizing

Even before the Arab Spring, U.S. policy in the Middle East was not in great shape. The Arab–Israeli peace process was moribund. U.S. relations with Israel were severely strained. Iran was still pursuing nuclear weapons and cracking down further on the Green Movement. Syria had neither been effectively isolated nor constructively engaged. Hezbollah had increased its governing stake in Lebanon. With the added mix of risks and opportunities of the Arab Spring, broad strategic rethinking is essential. Avoiding duck tests and their ABT, our SOB, and historical mis-analogy corollaries isn't all that is needed in such a process. But it sure would help.

Notes

1. Walter LaFeber, *Inevitable Revolutions: The United States in Central America* (New York: W.W. Norton & Company, 1993), pp. 115–116.
2. On the uses and misuses of history see Ernest R. May, *"Lessons" of the Past: The Use and Misuse of History in American Foreign Policy* (New York: Oxford University Press, 1973) and Richard E. Neustadt, *Thinking in Time: The Uses of History for Decision-Makers* (New York: Free Press, 1986).
3. Hans J. Morgenthau, "To Intervene or Not to Intervene," *Foreign Affairs* 45, no. 3 (April 1967): p. 434.
4. Encyclopedia of the New American Nation, "The Munich Analogy–The Vietnam War," http://www.americanforeignrelations.com/E-N/The-Munich-Analogy-The-vietnam-war.html.
5. President John F. Kennedy, "Address on the First Anniversary of the Alliance for Progress" (speech, the White House, Washington, D.C., March 13, 1962), http://www.presidency.ucsb.edu/ws/?pid=9100#axzz1LrGlsDJa; John F. Kennedy, "Announcing the Alliance for Progress" (speech, the White House, Washington, D.C., March 13, 1961), http://www.fordham.edu/halsall/mod/1961kennedy-afp1.html.
6. Abraham F. Lowenthal, *Partners in Conflict: The United States and Latin America* (Baltimore: Johns Hopkins University Press, 1987), p. 30.
7. U.S. Congress, House of Representatives, Permanent Select Committee on Intelligence, Subcommittee on Evaluation, *Iran: Evaluation of U.S. Intelligence Performance Prior to November 1978, Staff Report* (Washington, D.C.: U.S. Print Office, 1979), pp. 6–7.
8. Gary Sick, *All Fall Down: America's Tragic Encounter with Iran* (New York: Penguin Books, 1985), pp. 4, 148; Cyrus Vance, *Hard Choices: Critical Years in America's Foreign Policy* (New York: Simon and Schuster, 1983), p. 333; George Ball, *The Past Has Another Pattern* (New York: W.W. Norton, 1982), p. 460.
9. Zbigniew Brzezinski, *Power and Principle: Memoirs of the National Security Advisor 1977-1981* (New York: Farrar, Straus and Giroux, 1983), p. 394.

10.   Scott Sayare, "Zarzis Journal: Now Feeling Free, But Still Without Work, Tunisians Look Toward Europe," *New York Times*, March 24, 2011, http://query.nytimes.com/gst/fullpage.html?res=9B00E7DA1331F937A15750C0A9679D8B63&&scp=1&sq=It's%20an%20entire%20coutnry%20that%20needs%20to%20be%20remade&st=cse; Thomas Carothers, "Think Again: Arab Democracy," *Foreign Policy*, March 10, 2011, http://www.foreignpolicy.com/articles/2011/03/10/think_again_arab_democracy?page=0,0.

11.   United Nations Development Programme and Arab Fund for Economies and Social Development, *Arab Human Development Report 2002* (New York: United Nations, 2002), http://www.arab-hdr.org/publications/other/ahdr/ahdr2002e.pdf.

12.   United Nations Development Programme, *Arab Human Development Report 2009* (New York: United Nations, 2009), p. 116, http://www.arab-hdr.org/publications/other/ahdr/ahdr2009e.pdf.

13.   Mohammed Ayoob, *The Many Faces of Political Islam: Religion and Politics in the Muslim World* (Ann Arbor, MI: University of Michigan Press, 2008).

14.   Carrie Rosefsky Wickham, "The Muslim Brotherhood After Mubarak," *Foreign Affairs*, February 3, 2011, http://www.foreignaffairs.com/articles/67348/carrie-rosefsky-wickham/the-muslim-brotherhood-after-mubarak. See also Dina Guirguis, "Egypt after the Revolution: An Early Assessment," Washington Institute for Near East Policy, April 14, 2011, http://www.washingtoninstitute.org/templateC05.php?CID=3348; Scott Payne, "Egypt's Muslim Brotherhood and U.S. Interests," Third Way, February 23, 2011, http://www.thirdway.org/subjects/25/publications/375.

15.   Amr Hamzawy and Nathan J. Brown, "The Egyptian Muslim Brotherhood: Islamist Participation in a Closing Political Environment," Carnegie Endowment for International Peace, March 2010, p. 2, http://www.carnegieendowment.org/files/muslim_bros_participation.pdf.

16.   Daniel Byman, "Egypt 2012: What if the Muslim Brotherhood Comes to Power?" *Wall Street Journal*, February 4, 2011, http://blogs.wsj.com/ideas-market/2011/02/04/egypt-2012-what-if-the-muslim-brotherhood-comes-to-power/.

17.   Nathan Brown, "The Muslim Brotherhood," testimony before the House Permanent Select Committee on Intelligence, April 13, 2011, http://carnegieendowment.org/files/0413_testimony_brown.pdf.

18.   Steve Coll, "The Casbah Coalition," *The New Yorker*, April 4, 2011, pp. 34–40.

19.   Robert Winnett and Duncan Gardham, "Libya: Al-Qaeda Among Libya Rebels, NATO Chief Fears," *The Telegraph*, March 29, 2011, http://www.telegraph.co.uk/news/worldnews/africaandindianocean/libya/8414583/Libya-al-Qaeda-among-Libya-rebels-Nato-chief-fears.html; "Al Qaeda Bolstering Presence in Libya, Algeria Says," *Reuters Africa*, April 6, 2011, http://af.reuters.com/article/topNews/idAFJOE73504520110406.

20.   David E. Sanger and Eric Schmitt, "White House Assails Pakistan Effort on Militants," *New York Times*, April 5, 2011, http://www.nytimes.com/2011/04/06/world/asia/06pakistan.html?_r=1&ref=world.

21.   Dexter Filkins, "After the Uprising," *The New Yorker*, April 11, 2011, pp. 39–51.

22.   The Libyan Interim National Council, "Statement of the Transitional National Council on Counter-Terrorism," March 30, 2011, http://ntclibya.org/english/counter-terrorism/.

23.   Juan C. Zarate, "Al Qaeda Stirs Again," *New York Times*, April 17, 2011, http://www.nytimes.com/2011/04/18/opinion/18Zarate.html?_r=1&scp=9&sq=Zarate&st=cse.

24.   Steven Weber and Bruce W. Jentleson, *The End of Arrogance: America in the Global Competition of Ideas* (Cambridge, MA: Harvard University Press, 2010).

25. Sandeep Dikshit, "India Seeks a Relationship of Equals with U.S., Says Menon," *The Hindu*, November 3, 2010, http://www.hindu.com/2010/11/03/stories/2010110363411 600.htm.

26. Michael Crowley, "White Hot Bosporus," *New Republic*, April 29, 2010, p. 8.

27. Hal Brands, *Dilemmas of Brazilian Grand Strategy*, U.S. Army War College, Strategic Studies Institute, August 2010, http://www.strategicstudiesinstitute.army.mil/pubs/dis play.cfm?pubid=1017.

28. Michael Slackman, "Bullets Stall Youthful Push for Arab Spring," *New York Times*, March 17, 2011, http://www.nytimes.com/2011/03/18/world/middleeast/18youth.html? scp=1&sq=Slackman%20Bullets%20Stall&st=cse.

29. Ibid.

30. "'We Are All Hamad' Campaign to be Launched," Bahrain Online News, May 1, 2011, http://www.bahrainonlinenews.com/2011/05/we-are-all-hamad-campaign-to-be-launched/.

31. Pew Global Attitudes Project, "Egyptians Embrace Revolt Leaders, Religious Parties and Military, As Well," April 25, 2011, http://pewglobal.org/files/2011/04/Pew-Glob al-Attitudes-Egypt-Report-FINAL-April-25-2011.pdf.

32. "Bahrain: Gulf Troops to Stay as Counter to Iran," ArabNews.com, April 18, 2011, http://arabnews.com/middleeast/article364592.ece; "GCC Urges UN to Halt 'Inte rference' by Iran," *Khaleej Times*, April 19, 2011, http://www.khaleejtimes.com/dartic len.asp?xfile=data/middleeast/2011/April/middleeast_April401.xml&section=middleeast.

Mina Al-Oraibi and Gerard Russell

The Trust Deficit: Seven Steps Forward for U.S.– Arab Dialogue

"We are in an information war…and we are losing," declared U.S. Secretary of State Hillary Clinton, describing U.S. efforts to counter extremists and engage Arab publics during this year's unprecedented and historic change in the Middle East.[1] She is right. In the decade since 9/11, thousands of American lives and more than a trillion dollars have been spent on wars in Iraq and Afghanistan, while millions of dollars have been spent on public diplomacy programs aimed at the Arab world. In 2009, President Barack Obama delivered a landmark speech in Cairo designed to seek "a new beginning between the United States and Muslims around the world."[2] Two years on, according to the latest polling data in Egypt, unfavorable views of the United States outnumber favorable ones by nearly four to one.[3] With some exceptions, the United States likewise remains unpopular in most majority-Muslim countries from Morocco to Pakistan. Why? And what can be done about it?

The information war matters more than the war of bullets. Osama bin Laden is dead, but the real battle that must be won is against his ideas. In such a battle, public communications are key. As events in Tunisia, Egypt, and elsewhere have shown, public opinion can shape the region in surprising ways—ways that affect the United States directly, as prices at the gasoline pumps are showing. For these practical reasons, even aside from motives of common humanity, the United States needs to be engaging with the Arab world more effectively.

Mina Al-Oraibi is the Washington, D.C. Bureau Chief for *Asharq Al-Awsat*, the world's largest pan-Arab daily newspaper. She can be reached at Mina.aloraibi@gmail.com. Gerard Russell is a Research Fellow at the Harvard Kennedy School of Government. He can be reached at gerard_russell@hks.harvard.edu.

Copyright © 2011 Center for Strategic and International Studies
The Washington Quarterly • 34:3 pp. 151–163
DOI: 10.1080/0163660X.2011.588168

Osama bin Laden is dead, but the battle that must be won is against his ideas.

In this article, we draw on our experiences in government and journalism to set out seven ways in which the United States can win the war of ideas in the Middle East. Hundreds of articles have addressed this issue, but this article is unusual by addressing it from a practitioner's perspective. One of us has spent much of the past ten years explaining Western policies to Middle Eastern audiences, including for two years as Tony Blair's spokesman to global Muslim audiences. The other has been reporting on them for the world's largest pan-Arab daily newspaper, *Asharq Al-Awsat*, and is now that newspaper's Washington correspondent.

Several officials and opinion formers that we spoke to for this article, including former U.S. diplomats, told us that the fundamental reason for America's unpopularity was the nature of its policies, not the way they were presented. They suggested that few Arabs would respect the United States while they remember photos of Abu Ghraib, read accounts of detentions at Guantanamo, and can see that peace has not been achieved between Israelis and Palestinians. Take the view of Jamal Khashooggi, the editor-in-chief of Al-Waleed, the Arab world's newest satellite TV station: "America must understand that the Middle East conflict is the mother of all problems...the other issue is the American military presence in Iraq and Afghanistan." Apart from anything else, the experience of colonization in the 20th century makes this military presence especially controversial: "it is insulting to (our) people's mind, the Americans thought we are like Japan or Germany after the Second World War, yet they didn't have the history we have."[4]

This view implies that public diplomacy and the information war don't matter. In our view, however, communicating with the Arab world should be a two-way process: aiming to influence Arab public opinion, but also learning from it to potentially shape the policies themselves.

Seven Principles for Progress

It's Not About Religion, Stupid

President Obama's June 4, 2009 speech in Cairo was a tour de force. It achieved a huge boost in America's popularity in the Middle East and beyond. And yet, it made a basic mistake. By focusing on religion—"Islam" was mentioned 26 times and "Muslim" 48 times—it re-emphasized a false dichotomy between Islam and the West, a view that assumes that the principal source of tension between the United States and the Middle East is religious.

Practical moves by the U.S. government have followed a similar pattern—appointing a Special Representative to Muslim Communities, for example. Choosing one person to link the United States to more than one billion Muslims in both Muslim-majority countries and non-majority countries (such as New Zealand and Canada) gives an indication that the United States sees Muslims as being different solely based on religion. No other religion has been assigned this status in U.S. foreign policy.

> Communicating should be a two-way process, shaping Arab public opinion but also U.S. policies.

Of course, there are similarities in attitude between people in a range of Muslim-majority countries from Morocco to Pakistan, but these are not shared by all Muslims worldwide: attitudes in Indonesia and Malaysia, and indeed in Iran, remain somewhat different. Kosovar Muslims have erected a statue to Bill Clinton and named their children after Tony Blair. Embassies and desk officers in the State Department or U.S. intelligence agencies take great care to understand the differences between Middle Eastern countries (as was highlighted in the cables leaked by WikiLeaks in November 2010), but these are not sufficiently reflected in either public statements or outreach efforts.

Aiming outreach efforts at Muslims excludes citizens of those countries who are not Muslim, or whose primary identity is not their religion. Ali Asani, professor of Indo-Muslim and Islamic Religion and Cultures at Harvard University, regards the term "Muslim world" as "dehumanizing": it reduces diverse human beings to the single common denominator of their religious beliefs.[5]

Religion is also a particularly sensitive issue, and easily mishandled. Iraq is a prime example. In the run-up to the 2003 invasion, and even to the present day, U.S. officials refer to Iraqis as Sunni, Shia, and Kurds. The first two are religious groups while the third is ethnic, so this is already an erroneous mix of religious and ethnic divisions. Furthermore, when the United States and its allies based their outreach to Iraqis on these labels, many Iraqis felt that they were being divided and conquered. Although U.S. officials quickly dismiss the notion, this was in fact a tactic used in colonial times and remains vivid in the collective memory of many people of the region.

Finally, it would be a mistake to assume that the most important motivators for anger at the United States are religious. Osama bin Laden's propaganda focused on U.S. policies far more than theology. As journalist and al-Qaeda expert Peter Bergen told us: "It's the politics, stupid."[6]

Drop "Moderates versus Extremists"

Along with the religious handle has come another false dichotomy: that between "moderates" and "extremists." The way that these terms are used, it is often unclear what "moderates" are moderate about. Put the word in a different context, and it may be clearer: what is a moderate Christian? Does it mean someone who votes for mainstream political parties, or someone who accepts gay marriage, or just someone who rejects the use of violence against abortion clinics? The term when used about Muslims is similarly confusing.

> The Cairo speech was a tour de force, but made a basic mistake by focusing on religion.

It is also detrimental to the alliances that the United States wants to forge. The term "moderate Muslims" has negative connotations when translated into Arabic, and therefore labeling leaders as such is problematic. It conveys the idea of their being weak in their faith and not devoted to their religion, thus delegitimizing them in the eyes of their people. Moreover, moderate also holds connotations of being lukewarm in temperament and thus not committed to a certain belief. Surely, the United States does not want "moderate" support or alliances, rather than those built on strong beliefs and steadfast trust.

The implication of this use of language is that Muslims are assumed guilty until branded as moderate. This approach was largely born out of President George W. Bush's statement that "Either you are with us, or you are with the terrorists." But the people that the United States aims to win over are neither extremist nor moderate—they are the often silent majority that provides the oxygen to any ideology which will ferment into action, either positive or negative.

So the labels of extremism and moderation are incorrect and unhelpful. Instead, the United States should use the paradigm of confronting instability and crime. For example, Somalia suffers from organized crime and a lack of government which allows for criminal gangs to roam the streets of Mogadishu. Al-Qaeda has taken advantage of the situation as criminal gang leaders lure young, hopeless men by giving themselves the branding of religion through groupings like al-Shabab, the insurgent group fighting in Somalia. When U.S. officials echo this religious branding in their own public statements—referring to al-Shabab solely as religious extremists—they're unwittingly legitimizing them.

Most officials in the Obama administration were cautious in using these controversial terms during the uprisings in the Middle East that kicked off in Tunisia and Egypt at the start of this year. Moreover, U.S. officials were rightly emphasizing the unique nature of each country in public statements. Yet, in defining regional developments while addressing the pro-Israeli, pro-peace group J Street, President Obama's special assistant Dennis Ross said "change in Egypt has created concern for many in the region; Egypt has been a pillar of Israel's pursuit of peace. The last thing we want is to see extremists benefit from the situation."[7] Ross, who is instrumental in planning the White House's Middle East policies, raised the issue of "extremism," rather than calling on whoever comes to power in Egypt to respect international agreements and secure peace for their people and beyond. Brandishing one grouping or another as extremist will only alienate them and embolden their supporters.

Engage with Regional Media

As of the writing of this article, there has not yet been a single White House, National Security Agency, or State Department briefing specifically for Arab journalists on what the U.S. position is regarding the dramatic changes in the Middle East. In the last weekend of January, which witnessed the start of the revolution in Egypt, Secretary Clinton did six television interviews with U.S. news channels— but did not speak to a single Arab or African media outlet. This was followed much later by three short interviews Clinton conducted with three Arab-language television stations, but they focused in large part on Iran. As Joseph Nye argues, "the foreign press corps has to be the most important target for the first dimension of public diplomacy."[8] In practice, the foreign press corps—specifically Arab, Afghan, and Pakistani journalists—is often forgotten.

> **"M**oderate" Muslim holds connotations of being lukewarm and not committed to one's faith.

There have been some exceptions. President Obama gave his first television interview as president to an Arab television channel, Al-Arabiya. After former Egyptian president Hosni Mubarak stepped down from power, Secretary Clinton conducted an interview with Masrawy.com, one of the most popular Web portals in Egypt: 7,000 questions were collected online and from Tahrir Square. The United States did a great job after 2001 in setting up media hubs in Dubai, London, and Brussels to interact with media on the ground, with spokespeople who were fluent in Arabic. Its softer campaigns, designed to promote U.S. values or prove that the United States treats its own Muslim citizens well, had their place and their usefulness too. And its use of new media—from sending out instant SMS messages of President Obama's Cairo speech to being active on Twitter and YouTube—has been exemplary. But none of this substitutes for what Arabs really want to see: policymakers engaging with them directly in public about U.S. policies in an honest and transparent manner. This is especially relevant with the wave of uprisings in the Arab world that highlight the disconnect between public opinion and officialdom in many parts of the region. For issues where the United States is adopting policies that it knows will not sit well with Middle Eastern audiences, it should at least try to explain the reasoning behind those policies, or help others, such as Arab journalists, to do so.

The vast majority of high-level background briefings at the White House which tackle regional issues and explain the nuances of U.S. policy are open only to U.S. press—excluding journalists from the region. When the United States was working with UN Security Council members at the end of 2010 to end the bulk of Chapter VII resolutions on Iraq, which dealt with sanctions imposed under Saddam Hussein's regime, it was U.S. journalists who were briefed about these efforts— while Arab journalists, the very ones who were going to be explaining these developments and their positive impact on Iraq to Arab readers, were excluded.

The United States could also benefit from more informal engagement with newspaper and television editors, so that those opinion shapers can better understand the U.S. view on key regional issues over the long term—not just quick interviews whose impact only lasts as long as a headline remains relevant. An awareness of the regional media's more practical needs will also help: for example, paying more attention to deadlines and time zones in the region. A rebuttal given at 4:00 p.m. Washington time to a story that broke at 8:00 a.m. Beirut time means all the news cycles in the region have spent the day reporting a story without U.S. input or response.

We are making these points with specific reference to the Arab media, but similar circumstances apply in Afghanistan. The United States does have a small number of soldiers and officials who can communicate effectively in Dari and Pashto, but they appear rarely on Afghan television to communicate directly with the Afghan public (no Afghan of our acquaintance has ever seen this happen). That's a pity: a report in late 2010 issued by the Open Society Foundations highlighted the "trust deficit" between the Afghan public and the international community, bloodily demonstrated by anti-foreigner riots after the burning of a Qur'an by Pastor Terry Jones in Florida in March.[9] Said Tayeb Jawad, former Afghan ambassador to the United States, told us that the Afghan public's concern on issues such as a planned gradual drawdown of U.S. forces in July this year, and the prospect of talks with the Taliban, needed to be addressed with "a clear public statement. . .crafted for people in Kabul, rather than Brussels or Washington."[10]

Don't Get Lost in Translation

Ambassador Ronald Neumann served in Iraq and Afghanistan. Now president of the American Academy of Diplomacy, he negotiated with tribal leaders in Fallujah in 2004, just before the Marines conducted operations there (an episode known as the Second Battle of Fallujah). An Arabic speaker himself, he nonetheless borrowed an interpreter from the Marine Corps Commander in order to make sure that no mistakes were made. But as he listened to the interpreter translating what he had said, he realized that vital parts of the message were being missed. Three times he had to interrupt to correct the translation. Interviewed for this article, he told us, "I have no idea how many people we have killed because we think we have told them something they haven't heard."[11]

If he had not been an Arabic speaker, he might well never have known that his message had been mistranslated. In 2003 in Basra, a British brigadier, trying to establish a working relationship with the Iraqis on the newly-created city council, was perplexed that they seemed to want to raise the issue of religion, when he simply wanted to reassure them that British troops "had come to Basra in good faith." He was not aware that the interpreter had translated his remark as "we have brought a good religion." He was lucky that the city council didn't consider this confused statement an attempt to convert them to Christianity.

As Neumann commented, interpreters frequently do not understand both Arabic and English with total fluency. Nor are many U.S. diplomats or soldiers trained in the use of interpreters (brief them beforehand on what you are going to say, use short sentences with no jargon, and pause often). Luckily, the United States has had a number of officials who were able to go on television and radio and give interviews in Arabic, especially after 2001. This gave opportunities for them to clarify issues where hostility to U.S. policies and behavior was founded on misunderstanding. Ana Escrogima, a State Department spokesperson in Dubai from 2007 to 2010, explains:

> I would not have been able to do the job the way I did it without Arabic. Just having the language skills to follow the media and the nuances in statements by political figures, scholars and opinion formers—to basically follow the conversations taking place on all levels—and that fed into how I can address issues…you have to also listen and learn to listen, as there is a respect shown in listening. Establishing that kind of rapport, even before uttering a single word about policy, creates openness to the message.[12]

People with such linguistic ability are few in the State Department. They are few, too, in the media and think-tank community. The result is that policymaking is heavily influenced by English-language sources and English speakers, almost all of whom belong to the well-educated elite. All too often, embassies get to know a certain group of prominent members of society and will engage with that select group, without taking time to open up the possibilities of new interlocutors. This has worrying effects not only on U.S. relations in many countries, but also limits gathering accurate and full information about a certain country.

The Ugly American, written in 1958, asked its readers to "think, for a moment, what it costs us whenever an official American representative demands that the native speak English, or be not heard."[13] When was the last time a political leader from the Middle East or Afghanistan who spoke no English got favorable attention in Washington or London? No wonder the popularity of fundamentalism and the discontents of the poor still pose a conundrum for policymakers in both capitals.

Be Persistent and Consistent

President Obama's 2009 Cairo speech about a "New Beginning" was a huge presentational success, articulating a number of positions of principle. But the implementation of those principles has been inconsistent, even down to revoking in effect the proposal to close the Guantanamo detention camp. The reason that the United States is polling so badly in much of the Muslim world may even be that the Cairo speech raised expectations—without the policy successes that its audience expected would follow. According to Gallup, the U.S. approval rating in Algeria, for example, in 2008 was 25 percent, went up to 43 percent at the end of 2009, only to drop to 30 percent by end of 2010. This pattern was noted by Gallup in all Middle East and North African countries where it carried out polling.[14] Shadi Hamid of the Brookings Doha Center told us that "The address seemed to promise a lot, but delivered very little in the subsequent months…which again underlined America's problem: the rhetoric is often quite good, but the policy follow-up never comes even close to matching the rhetoric."[15]

The United States faced a policy challenge this spring as popular uprisings in Tunisia, Egypt, and elsewhere drove autocratic governments, which were also U.S. allies, out of office. The U.S. public generally supported the demonstrators, especially when their peaceful protests were met in several cases with violence. But U.S. policymakers were more cautious, upping their rhetoric on Egypt, for example, only after President Mubarak left office.

This is understandable: the United States was protecting its alliances and its national interests. Uniquely, however, the United States is expected by its own people and others around the world to promote universal values. Several U.S. diplomats and officials pointed out to us that other influential foreign powers in the region, like France or China, are not held up to the same standard as the United States and not scrutinized in the same manner. This is entirely true, but it is not unfair. The United States has set higher standards for itself; since its officials speak out for liberty and human rights and the United States claims to have "values-based" policies, they must in turn truly stand for these values. Otherwise, their slogans will fall on deaf ears.

Nevertheless, there is a middle way, and there have been signs this spring that the United States wishes to pursue it. It entails limiting the expectations that many people have developed in the Middle East—to deflate the image of an omnipotent United States. Some former ambassadors suggested that one task of U.S. communicators should be to explain clearly and repeatedly that the U.S. system is not ruled by one man, as so many Arab countries are, but instead has multiple competing power centers.

U.S. officials also need to watch for messages that are either delivered differently to the Middle East or are understood differently there. One example relates to the United States ending its military operations and withdrawing its troops in Iraq by the end of 2011. While U.S. officials explained to a U.S. audience that they are intent on sticking to the timetable set out by the Status of Forces agreement, these officials have not communicated as effectively to Iraqi and Arab audiences. The policy line is to withdraw all troops unless the Iraqi government asks the United States to remain (this policy is asserted without reference as to why the United States would want to maintain a military presence if asked). This leads to instant suspicions that the United States may decide to maintain a military presence after 2011. Instead, an effort should be made to explain U.S. interests in staying or leaving and how these relate to Iraq's interests in maintaining stability or supporting intelligence operations.

> The U.S. has correctly been deflating expectations and its image as omnipotent.

Taking a consistent and persistent approach might help dispel that bugbear of Westerners in the Middle East: the conspiracy theory. U.S. diplomats note that conspiracy theories will lay the blame on the United States for just about everything bad that happens. (If it's any consolation, Britain's been there too: in Iran to this day, Iranians accuse Britain of being the Ayatollahs' covert backer. In Afghanistan, Pashtuns say Britain is secretly sponsoring the drug trade. All of these stories, however unfounded they may seem today, often have a grain of historical truth.) Conspiracy theories aren't unique to the Middle East. As sociological studies show, they tend to flourish among people who are under stress, and who mistrust official news sources. They were common in the United States during World War II and at times of heightened racial tension in the 1960s.

The response that the authorities found worked best was to maintain a reputation for openness and truth-telling. Edward R. Murrow, the former Director of the U.S. Information Agency, explained in a May 1963 testimony before a congressional committee: "American traditions and the American ethic require us to be truthful, but the most important reason is that truth is the best propaganda and lies are the worst. To be persuasive we must be believable; to be believable we must be credible; to be credible we must be truthful. It is as simple as that."[16]

Don't Dodge the Issue

At the beginning of 2011, Arab states worked to introduce a UN resolution condemning Israeli settlement activity. The resolution was worded in line with policies that the United States publicly has supported in the past. The Obama administration was quick, however, to veto the resolution. Secretary Clinton stated that "we don't see action in the United Nations or any other forum as being helpful in bringing about that desired outcome" of a two-state solution.[17] This was the principal policy line that was repeated day after day by U.S. officials throughout a week of heated debate on the contentious U.S. position.

This was a mistake. U.S. officials should at least have taken the time to explain their policy. Instead, they refused to engage in a discussion of the details in the resolution, limiting their position to literally repeating just a couple of policy lines sent out to journalists via email or from the spokesperson's podium. With such a contentious issue, this does not suffice.

As a result of not explaining itself, the United States risked looking evasive. In its editorial on January 23, 2011, the *National* newspaper, the leading English-language daily based in Abu Dhabi, posed the following question: "Has the U.S. policy changed... or was it not being truthful about its policy?"[18] The latter is a view that is often espoused in the Arab world.

It would be better, in fact, to explain the policy even if it is unpalatable. This was Alastair Campbell's approach, as Tony Blair's media supremo, when tasked by Blair post-9/11 to put British voices on the Arab airwaves:

> When Labour won the 1997 election in Britain, we did it by reaching out to audiences that were traditionally suspicious or downright hostile. And that meant addressing their concerns head-on, and if we couldn't persuade them, at least make sure they knew what we had to say. 9/11 changed so much, and one thing it brought home to me is what a poor job all the main Western democracies had done in entering into a genuine dialogue with and about Islam. It meant that our opponents were able easily to get traction for hostile arguments against us and for conspiracy theories.[19]

Campbell wanted to put British faces on pan-Arab television, including the controversial Al-Jazeera channel, straight away:

> The key to strategic communications is being clear about your messages and communicating them in a clear and disciplined way, understanding that it takes time to put over a major point or argument. This was a section of the world that was suspicious of Britain and the United States, or even hostile, and bin Laden and his supporters were to a large extent dominating the Arab satellite media without anyone from Western governments being there to rebut him. We needed our people speaking Arabic, in the Arab media, tackling the contentious issues—the ones that

were making people angry—even if that meant that they would take some heat themselves.[20]

In engaging with non-governmental groups or political journalists, U.S. officials cannot hope to dodge discussion of policy issues. Key appointments have been made to address outside discontent with U.S. policies, for example the Under Secretary for Public Diplomacy and the Special Representative for Muslim Communities. Yet, the remit of these posts specifically excludes decisionmaking on policy concerns of the same audiences they are meant to be addressing. They are often the main officials, and usually the only officials, sent to speak with civil-society groups that often have misgivings about the United States from a policy angle specifically. Thus, not addressing the issues directly often weakens the impact of the serious efforts U.S. public diplomacy officials exert and alienates potential allies or supporters in any given country.

Work through Allies

Putting diplomats on television was the right thing to do; but it isn't the only, or even the best, way to change people's opinions. The best way that opinions can be changed in Middle Eastern societies is through their own internal debates— led, of course, by their own opinion-formers. Most experts that we talked to for this article suggested that their first priority would be to find, in Ambassador Neumann's words, "Who has credibility with the local audience and what is the best way to win understanding from them?"[21] Such people might be editors, journalists, playwrights, poets, or (most obviously, perhaps) politicians seen by the audience as sympathetic.

The United States cannot expect the people of the Middle East to echo its views and support its policies without reservation. It cannot put words in their mouths. This means, though, that the U.S. government's capacity to encourage democratic and liberal trends in Arab society is very limited. In Cairo in January 2011, both anti-government and pro-government protesters claimed that the other side was backed by the United States; as Stephen Grand of the Brookings Institution puts it, it is as if the United States has the reverse Midas touch.[22] What the United States can do, though, is encourage other governments to play a role in encouraging democracy and liberalism. For one thing, this means the European Union increasing its engagement with the region.

It also means that the United States can take comfort from the public relations successes of Turkey. Once mistrusted amongst most of the Arab world due to lingering resentment from the times of the Ottoman Empire and the era of Mustafa Kemal Ataturk, the last decade has witnessed an unprecedented improvement in Arab–Turkish relations. From lifting visa restrictions to exporting soap operas dubbed in Arabic, Turkey has infiltrated the homes and minds of millions of Arabs. This is coupled with a foreign policy that is directed at securing Turkey's position in the region as king-maker and friend to all sides. While Turkey's historic alliance with Israel continues to be a significant aspect of its foreign policy of its foreign policy, Ankara's open criticism of the Gaza and Lebanon wars earned it much support.

Of course, the United States cannot follow the exact same foreign policy, and Turkey's geographical location and majority-Muslim population means that it has certain advantages that the United States will never have. One lesson can be learned, however, from Prime Minister Recep Tayyip Erdogan's Chief Advisor Ibrahim Kalin, who is also the Chief Public Diplomacy Official. Kalin explains that "we have an increasing capacity for soft power...our policy is both principled and pragmatic," adding that "mutual empowerment" is key.[23] This means that people of the region know that when Turkey strengthens economic ties, it is to strengthen both Turkish business and local businesses; the same applies to forging political allegiances or giving aid.

The United States Still Uniquely Matters

This article has addressed itself entirely to the United States. That is because of its unparalleled ability to influence the Middle East for good or ill (although this unique status is not guaranteed, especially with the changes sweeping the region). Leaving aside its programs of assistance and military cooperation, there is a question here of moral leadership. For as long as the United States, the world's premier liberal democracy, remains unpopular, it has a chilling effect on those within the Middle East who favor democracy and liberal values. There is a compelling need to bridge the trust deficit in U.S. relations with the people of the region. If they do not see Americans defending or explaining their own policies, they are less likely to speak out themselves. The United States—its government and people—must therefore find its voice in the Middle East, and open its ears. If it starts by following these seven principles, it can move in that direction.

Notes

1. Secretary of State Hillary Clinton, "National Security & Foreign Policy Priorities in the FY 2012 International Affairs Budget," testimony before the Senate Foreign Relations Committee, March 2, 2011.
2. President Barack Obama, "Remarks by the President on a New Beginning" (speech, Cairo University, Cairo, Egypt, June 4, 2009), http://www.whitehouse.gov/the-press-office/remarks-president-cairo-university-6-04-09.
3. Pew Global Attitudes Project, "Egyptians Embrace Revolt Leaders, Religious Parties and Military, As Well," April 25, 2011, http://pewglobal.org/files/2011/04/Pew-Global-Attitudes-Egypt-Report-FINAL-April-25-2011.pdf.

4. Interview with authors, World Economic Forum Annual Meeting, Davos, Switzerland, January 2011.
5. Interview with authors, May 2010.
6. Interview with authors, January 2011.
7. Dennis Ross, remarks at "J Street Conference 2011," Washington, D.C., February 28, 2011.
8. Joseph S. Nye, Jr., *Soft Power: The Means To Success In World Politics* (New York: PublicAffairs, 2004).
9. Open Society Foundations, "The Trust Deficit: The Impact of Local Perceptions on Policy in Afghanistan," October 7, 2010, http://www.soros.org/initiatives/mena/articles_publications/publications/policy-afghanistan-20101007/perceptions-20101007.pdf.
10. Interview with authors, May 2011.
11. Interview with authors, January 2011.
12. Interview with authors, Washington, D.C., January 2011.
13. Eugene Burdick and William J. Lederer, *The Ugly American* (New York: W.W. Norton & Company, 1999).
14. Gallup, "U.S. Approval Gains Nearly Erased in Middle East/North Africa," September 30, 2010, http://www.gallup.com/poll/143294/approval-gains-nearly-erased-middle-east-north-africa.aspx.
15. Interview with authors, January 22, 2011.
16. See: http://www.usdiplomacy.org/diplomacytoday/contemporary/public.php.
17. Secretary of State Hillary Clinton, remarks during a press event with Estonian Foreign Minister Urmas Paet, Washington, D.C., January 20, 2011.
18. Editorial in the *National*, January 23, 2011.
19. Interview with authors, January 2011.
20. Ibid.
21. Interview with authors, January 2011.
22. Interview with authors, January 2011.
23. Ibrahim Kalin, remarks made during the SETA Foundation's "Insight Turkey Annual Conference: Debating New Turkey," Washington, D.C., December 3, 2010.

WELCOME TO THE NEIGHBORHOOD

Every year, GW's Elliott School of International Affairs hosts more than 250 public events featuring hundreds of renowned policymakers, scholars, journalists, diplomats, and other world leaders.

Our unique location in the heart of Washington, D.C. enriches our teaching and research by giving our students and faculty unparalleled opportunities to engage with the international leaders who walk through our doors on a regular basis.

Learn more about our innovative undergraduate and graduate programs or view some of our superb special events online at www.elliott.gwu.edu.

CONNECTED TO THE WORLD
The Elliott School of International Affairs

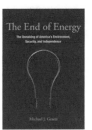

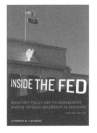